Researching Ramirez

Researching Ramirez

On the Trail of the Jesus Ramirez Family

Pamela Humphrey

ResearchingRamirez@gmail.com

ResearchingRamirez.com

ISBN-13: 978-1508796299

For my mom
and my boys

Contents

Introduction

This book started as a genealogy project – to write down the family history for the Ramirez branch of my mom's family to share with my boys, my mom, and those who had shared information about the family with me. It quickly grew beyond a list of names and dates into a collection of stories of lives lived, of families, and distant cousins.

In hopes of putting our ancestors into the context of their time, I studied Mexican history. I have learned more about Mexican history during this project than I ever learned in school. Learning history through the lens of this family's life and travels made it come alive.

If there was ever hope of finishing the project, I had to keep a narrow focus. There could be volumes written about the descendants of this Ramirez family, but this story focuses on the family that came up from Mexico and the first generation born in the United States. In just their lifetimes, the family spreads across many states.

Even if you are not a descendant of Jesus Ramirez, I think you will enjoy not only the story but also reading about the process of discovery. There are many tips and ideas for researching your own family tree.

I hope you enjoy reading the story of this family, learn something about the history of the time in which they lived, and develop an awareness of how your ancestors' choices shaped the life you live now.

Special Thanks

The heart of this book is the thread of stories and photos that breathes life into names on documents. Thank you to all those that shared photos, information or stories with me:

* Oscar Ramirez Jr, grandson of Dolores Ramirez Castañon
* Rose DeHoyos, granddaughter of Dolores Ramirez Castañon
* Michelle Perez, great granddaughter of Dolores Ramirez Castañon
* Gloria Munguia, granddaughter of Plutarco Ramirez
* Viola Gutierrez, granddaughter of Plutarco Ramirez
* Ninfa Garcia, granddaughter of Ramon Ramirez
* Dora Rodriguez, granddaughter of Ramon Ramirez
* Tillie Guiterrez, granddaughter of Ramon Ramirez
* Rosemary Piña, granddaughter of Leandro Ramirez
* Joe Maldonado, grandson of Leonor Ramirez Sarabia
* Yolanda Garza, granddaughter of Guillermo Ramirez
* Ernestine Andrada, daughter-in-law of Maria Suttles Andrada
* Lucinda Elizondo Anderson, granddaughter of Petra Rodriguez Elizondo
* Lucio Elizondo, grandson of Candida Torres Rodriguez
* Abraham Garcia, grandson of Candida Torres Rodriguez

* Brenda Alvarado, granddaughter of Herminda Guajardo Hernandez
* Peggy Ortiz, granddaughter of Elias Guajardo
* David Maldonado Jr, grandson of Emma Suttles Maldonado
* Belle Quinones, granddaughter of Francisco Guajardo
* Jill, great granddaughter of Tana Rodriguez Castillo
* Alice Velasco Cortez, granddaughter of Lidia Ramirez Urias
* David Aguirre, great grandson of Lidia Ramirez Urias
* David Torres Jr, grandson of Isabel Ramirez Zapata
* Yolanda Amado, daughter of Julian Ramirez
* Abelardo Ramirez, son of Julian Ramirez
* Olga Luce, daughter of Julian Ramirez
* Andrea Dahlberg, great granddaughter of Julian Ramirez
* Steve Ramirez, grandson of Julian Ramirez
* Sarah Laffoday, granddaughter of Julian Ramirez
* Michelle Perez Bolanos, great granddaughter of Alfredo Ramirez
* Katie Ramirez, daughter of Abel Ramirez
* Donald Ramirez, son of Grady Ramirez
* Virginia Garza, daughter of Otila Ramirez Padilla
* Monica Green, granddaughter of Pete Ramirez
* Melissa Ramirez, granddaughter of Pete Ramirez (& her dad, Gerald Ramirez)
* And to many others in the Facebook family history group

Special thanks to Yolanda Flores, Leo & Pat Castañon, and George Ramirez for always sharing memories of family (& recipes!)

Warm thanks for all those that joined our Facebook Family History group and shared stories, photos and facts!

To my mom, Norma Ramirez Banks, thank you for patiently answering my many, many questions and for all the details you remember. Many branches would not have been discovered had it not been for the names that you remembered. To my dad, Dan Banks, thank you for all the driving around and for scanning numerous photos. And extra thanks to you both for the many hours you entertained the boys while I met with people.

Thank you also to Esther and Julian Solis, neighbors and life-long friends of the Castañon family that lived on Arbor Place, for sharing stories and memories with my mom.

Thank you to my friend, Pamela, who encouraged me to write it all down and share these stories. And a huge thanks to Pamela and my friend, Becky, for helping with editing. All errors are my own.

Thank you, Homero Adame, for allowing use of your photos of El Potosí and for sharing bits of information about the village.

Huge thanks to my husband and boys!

I am enormously thankful for Herlinda "Linda" Castañon Ramirez and Herminia "Mina" Castañon Ramirez. My Aunt Linda kept many detailed ledgers. Looking through those old ledgers, we found more than sums. We found recipes, birth dates, death dates, and more. Thank you, Aunt Linda, for writing things down!

My grandma (Mina) kept contact with many first and second cousins; family was important. Thank you, Grandma, for letting my mom tag along when visiting so that she could remember people and tell me about them!

My grandma and Aunt Linda are referenced throughout this book. Because of their contacts, stories, photos, and notes this story was made possible. Those were the launching point for all that came after.

1

El Potosí

This story began in Mexico in a small town called El Potosí in the municipality of Galeana in the state of Nuevo León. El Potosí is just west of the southern end of the Sierra Madre Oriental Mountain Range. It sits in the high plains adjacent to mountains that were covered in pine-oak forests. In El Potosí there was a hacienda; historical references to Hacienda El Potosí noted that it was constructed about 1690 and was agricultural. It also worked livestock, possibly cattle or sheep. A large cluster of small adobe homes line wide dirt streets near the hacienda. In the village near the hacienda is a white adobe chapel with a bell tower. Near the chapel is a small plaza; not far from the chapel is a hill with a tiny chapel-like structure on top where the *hacendados*[1] were buried. The chapel still stands and a handful of residents still populate the small village.

Our ancestors likely lived on corn (maize), beans, chiles, and squash. The tiny adobe homes had little or no furniture; the family slept on mats or on the dirt floor wrapped in their *serape* or *rebozo*[2]. Food was probably prepared outdoors. Corn was soaked, ground, shaped, and cooked to make corn tortillas – a staple of their diet.

---

[1] Hacienda owners

[2] A *rebozo* is a long scarf traditionally worn by Mexican women; a *serape* is a colorful woolen shawl worn over the shoulders, traditionally worn by Mexican men.

It is possible that they had only the clothes on their backs. Whatever they did not grow, they either received or purchased from the hacienda. Workers at the hacienda often received a portion of corn as part of their wages. The hacienda also had a store where villagers could purchase items. In some haciendas the store sold things at reasonable prices or prices lower than in the cities; other haciendas would overcharge for items because they had a monopoly on the market for that area.

In the area around Galeana, there were two large haciendas, but not any small private ranches. There are references to Indian families farming arid land in small plots on the sides of mountains. Was that the way our family scraped out a living?

Little was recorded about that hacienda and area. However, a few articles and stories do mention the Hacienda El Potosí. One reference was about an incident during the US-Mexican War (1846-1848). A Mexican military figure, Mariano Escobeda, captured some *"norte americanos"* and took them to the hacienda to turn them over to the local government. Another reference told of an Indian attack on El Peñuelo, a town near El Potosí, and part of the large hacienda properties. Forces from Galeana organized in El Potosí and went to El Peñuelo to recover bodies and find out what had happened. Indian attacks were part of the rural life that our ancestors lived.

History Snapshot 1: The chapel in El Potosí; Photo by Homero Adame, from his book "Haciendas del Altiplano, historias(s) y leyendas

History Snapshot 2: The chapel in El Potosí; Photo by Homero Adame, from his book "Haciendas del Altiplano, historias(s) y leyendas

This was the backdrop for the first part of our story. The marriages and christenings recorded took place in the simple white chapel. Every christening, marriage and funeral cost them a few pesos. Was the priest in El Potosí kind, humble, and generous charging only enough to get by? Or did he charge high prices for the sacraments in order to line his pockets?

In the records in Mexico, Ramirez was recorded as Ramires. Many other names, Gutierres, Cortes, and Gonsales were all written with an 's' instead of a 'z.' The name Ramirez was not written with a 'z' until after the family moved to Texas.

On 18 Sep 1848 Jesus Ramires married Maria de Jesus Perales ("Jesusa") in the small chapel in El Potosí in the parish of San Pablo, Galeana, Nuevo León, Mexico. Imagine 18-year old Jesusa dressed in her best (or only) dress, with a rebozo draped over her head, barefoot, maybe holding a handful of wild flowers that a younger sibling had picked for her. What was she thinking as she walked down the narrow aisle toward the altar and toward her groom, 28-year old Jesus? Did she have any inkling that her life would take her far away from her little village? Imagine Jesus, serape draped over his shoulder, smiling as his bride joined him at the front of the small white chapel while family and friends watched nearby. What were his hopes for the future? He was older than most other men typically married. Had he been away at war?

The priests recorded this marriage and other christenings, weddings, and deaths in elaborate script in books that are still legible and available for genealogy research on familysearch.org and Ancestry.com.

These records are one of the few sources for finding out more about our ancestors in Mexico. The Catholic records give us a lot of information. In the record for this marriage, there is a notation in the margin, "de Potosi." "De potosi" translates to "of Potosi" or "from Potosi." This is how we know that they were from El Potosí. The marriage record also lists the parents' names of the bride and groom. Jesus' parents are listed as Jose Maria Ramires and Clara Gutierres. Maria de Jesus' parents are listed as Cayetano Perales and Gertrudis Rosas.

Knowing the parents' names, we should be able to find christening records for the bride and groom and, hopefully, marriage records for their parents. Many of the records have been indexed so we can easily search the index rather than scanning through hundreds of pages of fanciful script written in old Spanish[3].

We search for Maria de Jesus Perales, born in San Pablo, Galeana, Nuevo León, Mexico, about 1830. We find a match. The father is Cayetano (sometimes spelled Calletano). The index gives us some information, but looking at the original is even better. So with the date and location shown in the index entry we start looking through pages in the Catholic records for the actual entry recorded by the priest.

Records were kept by parish, so we look in the Nuevo León Catholic records, in the municipality of Galeana, and the parish of

---

[3] Familysearch.org allows you to browse scans of the actual books and see the entries the priests recorded.

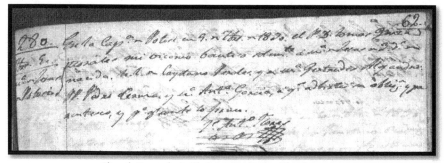

Church Records 1: Christening Record for Jesusa -
México, Nuevo León, registros parroquiales, 1667-1981, images, FamilySearch
(https://familysearch.org/pal:/MM9.3.1/TH-1-159380-121557-
84?cc=1473204&wc=MCMV-LP8:45389301,45389302,45452001 : accessed 27 Jun
2014), Galeana > San Pablo > Bautismos 1821-1833 > image 289 of 496.

San Pablo. On page 289 in the book of *Bautismos*[4] 1821-1833, we find the record!

It is a little hard to read, but we can make out some useful information. The beginning of the christening record records where the christening took place - in the chapel in El Potosí. After that, it records the date – 5 September 1830[5]. The priest, Tomas Garza Morales, christened her. It gives her name, how many days old she was when she was christened, her parents' names, and the names of her *padrinos*, or godparents. Her name is abbreviated as Ma de Jesus. Ma is a common abbreviation for Maria in the Catholic records. Curiously, her parents are listed as Cayetano Perales and Gertrudis Alejandro. Her marriage record lists her mother as Gertrudis Rosas.

Next, we search for Jesus Ramires, born in San Pablo about 1820, but we get no matches. Familysearch.org has a great search tool that allows you to search by different combinations of information. So we search using the information that we know. We

---

[4] *Bautismos* are Baptisms, or Christenings

[5] Septiembre (Spanish for September) is sometimes abbreviated 7bre. The pattern continues October through December. Oct is abbreviated 8bre, Nov is abbreviated 9bre, and Dec is abbreviated 10bre.

know the names of his parents so we search for a Jesus (no last name), born in San Pablo about 1820 whose parents are Jose Maria Ramires and Clara Gutierres. We still get no matches. So we put the search for Jesus' christening record on hold and search for a marriage record for his parents.

We enter the names Jose Maria Ramires and Clara Gutierres, but no records match. Remembering that Gertrudis' last name was different in the christening and the marriage record, we search by first names only – Jose Maria and Clara. We limit the search to San Pablo for a marriage during the years around 1820 because we know Jesus was born about 1820. The results show a marriage for a Jose Maria Alejandro and Clara Vega in 1819. Could they be the right people? Did they even have a son named Jesus?

To find the answer, we utilize the flexibility of the search tool again. Leaving names and birth fields blank, we search entering only a location of San Pablo and parents' names of Jose Maria Alejandro and Clara Vega. The results include no Jesus. However, Clara's last name is listed as Gutierres in her son's marriage record, so we search again using Jose Maria Alejandro and Clara Gutierres. A Jose Cipriano de Jesus Alejandro christened on 21 May 1820 is in the listed results. Could he be our Jesus Ramires?

Church Records 2: Christening Record for Jesus -
México, Nuevo León, registros parroquiales, 1667-1981, images, FamilySearch (https://familysearch.org/pal:/MM9.3.1/TH-1-159380-122295-87?cc=1473204&wc=MCMV-KWG:45389301,45389302,45422401 : accessed 02 Jun 2014), Galeana > > San Pablo > Bautismos 1787-1820 > image 374 of 392.

We look at his actual christening record. Everything looks like our Jesus Ramires was actually named Jose Cipriano de Jesus Alejandro when he was born. Can we find proof that these are the same people? Instead of spending frustrating hours chasing proof, we put this aside hoping we find something that can change our hunch to a proven fact.

We move on to scanning death records hoping to find death dates for any family that died in El Potosí. They have not yet been indexed so we need to browse page by page. We recognize the name of the mother on a death record – Maria de Jesus Perales. We know from other searches, discussed later, that Jesus Ramires and Maria de Jesus Perales christened a daughter, Maria de San Juan, in 1851. Now we are looking at a death record that shows a Maria de San Juan, daughter of Jose de Jesus Alejandro and Maria de Jesus Perales who died of a fever in 1852. This is our confirmation that the two people, Jose Cipriano de Jesus Alejandro and Jesus Ramires, are the same person.

No stories of changed names passed down through the family. This search started as a search of my Ramirez roots so learning that the surname was Alejandro before it was Ramirez is very much unexpected. Several of Jesus' siblings, christened as Alejandro were married as Ramires. A brother, Felipe, married as Felipe Ramires, but then later used the name Alejandro again when his children were christened.

It is unknown why Jose Cipriano de Jesus Alejandro changed his name to Jesus Ramires. Possible reasons suggested for the name change were: (1) someone with the Alejandro surname was in trouble or causing trouble and others changed their name to distance themselves, (2) a sister of Jesus was unmarried but having children and other family chose to disassociate, (3) the Indian culture did not find their identity in a surname; names were more fluid, and names from generations past were often adopted without cause, or (4) they chose a name that sounded more Spanish.

The idea that someone was running from something was brought up and then dismissed because the name changes all happened in this very small village where everyone knew each other. There was no hiding by just using a different surname.

We know that Jesus and Jesusa married in El Potosí. Did they have children there? We search the christening records using parents' names and San Pablo, Galeana, Nuevo León, Mexico, as the location to find any children christened in El Potosí who list

Jesus Ramires and Maria de Jesus Perales as parents. We enter San Pablo rather than El Potosí because San Pablo is the name of the parish. El Potosí is a small town within that parish. We learn that Jesus and Jesusa had four children while they lived in El Potosí:

- Porfiria - christened on 22 Sep 1849.
- Maria de San Juan - christened on 22 Jan 1851.
- Jesus Maria - christened on 3 Jun 1853.
- Petra - christened on 4 Jun 1856.

Sometime between Jun 1856 and Jun 1860, Jesus and Jesusa packed up their young family and moved away from El Potosí. Why and how, we wonder.

History Snapshot 3: El Potosí; Photo by Homero Adame,
from his book "Haciendas del Altiplano, historias(s) y leyendas

2

Saltillo

Was it with trepidation that Jesus and Jesusa packed their belongings? Their families had lived in the small village of El Potosí, working for the hacienda for generations. It was all that they had ever known. Was all they'd ever known not enough anymore? Was it desperation or a dream of something more that prompted the Ramires family to leave the only place and way of life they'd ever known and move to Saltillo?

The family probably did not have a wagon. It is possible that they had a *burro*[6] to carry their goods across the rocky paths to Saltillo, but most likely they gathered their possessions in bundles and strapped them to the backs of all but the youngest travelers.

The last child born in El Potosí was Petra, christened in June of 1856. Her younger sister, Manuela, was born in Jun 1860 in Saltillo. Sometime during that window of time, the family obviously moved to Saltillo.

Saltillo sits northwest of El Potosí in a wide valley flanked by the Zapaliname Mountains (part of the Sierra Madre Orientals.) It was founded in 1577, making it the oldest post-conquest city in northern Mexico. By 1860, it was a city full of abode homes and businesses.

The Guajardo family (see the Associated Families Chapter) also moved to Saltillo from El Potosí about the same time. Travelling in a large group offered safety from bandits, so the families likely

---

[6] donkey

travelled together. The Guajardo's son, Lucio, was born in El Potosí in Dec 1857. They probably did not travel in winter or fall; fall was the rainy season. During the rainy season many roads were impassable. So sometime in the spring or summer of 1858 or 1859 the families made the journey to their new life.

Felipe Alejandro, brother of Jesus Ramires, and his family also moved to Saltillo, but the timeframe is unclear. Agapita Ramires, sister of Jesus Ramires, and her husband, Navor Lara, also moved their family to Saltillo sometime between May 1859 and May 1861.

When the Ramires family made the journey, Porfiria was about nine, little Jesus was about five, and Petra was two or three years old. It must have been a long, adventurous week for the young family. Imagine the family looking down into the wide valley and seeing the large expanse dotted with adobe buildings. Was it exciting or frightening to see a city as large and busy as Saltillo after living in such a small village?

To learn about their time in Saltillo, we search through records. In our previous searches, we entered a location of San Pablo. Now we change that and search in Saltillo, Coahuila, Mexico. Entering the location and parents' names, Jesus Ramires and Maria de Jesus Perales, we see all the children christened in Saltillo.

But there are more records that we can search. Beginning about 1860, municipalities began recording civil records. These were very much like the Catholic records. These records are available for browsing at familysearch.org. We look through the civil records for Saltillo. The civil records provide information not given in the christening record. Civil records usually include the residence of the family. For one child, Mariana, we find her name as Josefa in the civil record.

Based on what we find, we know that their family expanded in Saltillo:

- Manuela was christened on 18 Jun 1860 in Sagrario Metropolitno, Saltillo, Coahuila, Mexico.
- Mariana was christened on 19 Mar 1862, but Josefa was listed in the Saltillo civil records born in Mar 1862.

Josefa or Josefin were listed on later census records. It seems these two are one and the same.

- Austacio was listed on the 1880 census with his parents, but a christening record for him has not been found. According to censuses, he was born about 1864.
- Gregorio was christened on 26 May 1866.
- Ignacio was christened on 21 Aug 1868.
- Plutarco was christened on 30 Jun 1870.
- Jesus and Jesusa adopted a little Indian girl, Estefana.[7]

Looking through the civil records, we find that in 1868, just a few weeks before Ignacio was born, Gregorio died of a fever. The civil death record lists their residence as *"Meson de Belen[8]."* A search for information about Meson de Belen lets us know that it is in the city center, not on the outskirts. Now we know that they were not farming on the outskirts of Saltillo. They were living in the heart of the city. Ignacio's civil birth record dated two months later lists their residence as *"Meson de San Julian."* Searches turn up very little about either location.

Our family was probably not a middle or upper income family. They were an Indian/mestizo family that had left possible debt peonage on the hacienda and relocated to Saltillo. Indian families that moved into the city often lived in or near poverty. Many took very few meals at home as there was usually no room for cooking appliances in the crowded rooms. Meals of corn tortillas, beans, and chile made with inexpensive cuts of meat (or fat!) were purchased from street vendors or restaurants. Tortillas were their only utensils.

As a means of support, some of the family learned trades or skills and sold their goods on the street. Hats or shoes might be carried on their backs or set up on a street corner. Others may have worked in factories. Later records noted that the younger Jesus was a shoemaker. Was that skill learned while he grew up in Saltillo?

---

[7] There are no records in Saltillo that record the adoption, but both family stories and records in Texas indicate that Estefana was adopted while they were in Saltillo.

[8] Meson de Belen literally translates to Inn of Bethlehem.

Their move to Saltillo happened during a tumultuous time in Mexico. Liberals took control of the government in 1855 and passed laws in hopes of creating modern economic growth. The first of the Reform Laws was decreed on Nov 23, 1855; the *Ley Juarez* (Juarez Law) established equality under the law and eliminated special courts for military, clergy, and other special interest groups. The *Ley Lerdo* (Lerdo law) passed in June 1856. It prohibited the church or civil organizations from owning or administering property not used in the everyday. The Catholic Church was required to sell off the properties they owned except for churches, monasteries, and seminaries. This law also affected the communal lands held by Indian villages. The last, the *Ley Iglesias* (The Iglesias Law[9]), adopted in Jan 1857, regulated parish fees, which prevented the clergy from charging exorbitant fees for christenings, marriages, and funerals. These laws were reinforced with the Constitution of 1857. The Constitution also had other provisions; debt peonage was abolished.

Benito Juarez took office in 1858, but since the conservatives controlled Mexico City, Juarez set up his government on the run. The bitter and bloody War of Reform started in 1858 and lasted three years. The Liberals gained popular support for their ideals and eventually won the war. After charging high fees for sacraments for many years, the Church had not gained favor with rural parishioners. The Church was strongly allied with the Conservatives.

By 1861, the War of Reform was over, but shortly after, the French "intervened." Maximillian was set up as king by the monarchists and again Benito Juarez was acting as President on the move. For six years, Benito Juarez moved around the country (and was in Saltillo for a time) while Mexico fought against the French forces. The French controlled much of Mexico by early 1865 and Maximillian declared that any Mexican fighting his empire would be shot.

The politics of the era influenced our family and they most certainly had opinions and beliefs about it, just as we do today.

---

[9] *Iglesias* means churches

Stories have passed down through the family about the younger Jesus. He was politically outspoken and protested in favor of Benito Juarez. One story was that he was being sought by the "*federales*" and his mother, Jesusa, hid him in the pig sty. In light of the political atmosphere during that time, it was likely that outspoken political protests would attract the interest of armed soldiers. His mother and those pigs probably saved his life.

We don't know why the family moved to Saltillo from El Potosí. Was it related to the changes of the time? Did the passage of the Reform Laws affect communal land holdings that they farmed or release them from debt peonage? After 12-14 years in Saltillo, the family was moving again, leaving Mexico - headed for Texas.

The Ramires family loaded their belongings into a wagon and left Saltillo. We know based on census records in Texas that Jesus and Jesusa made the journey with Jesus' mother Clara, their children, their adopted daughter, and possibly two of the Guajardo boys. Were they chasing hope – headed to the land of opportunity or were they leaving turmoil behind?

Benito Juarez died in July 1872. Was this part of the reason they left Mexico?

3

Texas

About 1872, the Ramirez family and those travelling with them packed their meager belongings into a wagon and left for Texas. They journeyed from Saltillo through Piedras Negras, Mexico, and Eagle Pass, Texas, into Guadalupe County near Seguin, Texas. Wagons travelled about 10 miles a day. The journey likely took the family forty-five days or more.

Seguin is the county seat and largest city in Guadalupe County, Texas. The county was settled about 1838 by soldiers awarded with land after Texas won its independence. It was a very rural area, and the two major occupations (for those living outside the city) were farming and livestock. From 1870 – 1910 this area saw a large influx of people from different countries, but more from Mexico than any other county. Many of these immigrants worked on cotton farms as laborers, sharecroppers, or tenant farmers. After the abolition of slavery just a few years before, there was a need for workers. Our ancestors likely stepped in to do the work previously done by slaves.

Was Guadalupe County the destination they had in mind when they left Saltillo? Had someone else they knew moved to the area earlier and sent word back? They must have travelled through or near San Antonio, which was a bustling, growing city. Why did they continue to the more rural area near Seguin? Were they hoping to return to a life of farm labor like they'd had in El Potosí rather than an urban life like in Saltillo?

There are several places we can search to hopefully find a record of the family in Texas: census records, marriage records, death records, newspapers, tax records, and church records. The Catholic Church recorded christenings, marriages, and sometimes deaths for those that attended the Catholic Church. Death certificates were recorded in some places earlier than 1903, but starting then, the State of Texas required it. Ancestry.com has an extensive searchable database of newspapers, which includes many newspapers from the San Antonio area.

We start by searching for a census record in the 1880 census. All censuses are available at Ancestry.com. The 1880 and 1940 censuses are searchable on familysearch.org at no cost.

We enter the name Jesus Ramirez and add Maria de Jesus as the spouse, but we get no matching results. The census takers wrote down the information they heard when collecting information, but they didn't always spell it correctly. So we alter our search and search for names that are less likely to be misspelled. Petra is easy to spell, right? We enter Petra as the first name, but leave the last name blank. Ramirez is often badly misspelled. We add Jesus as the father and enter Guadalupe County as the location, because we know from family accounts where they lived. That search results in a promising record.

The resulting record: a Jesus Romeras that lives in Guadalupe County. Other people in the household are: Kasusa (wife); Hoseffa, Austacio, Stephano, Enassio, Petra, Blutucko (sons and daughters); Acuio, Samuel, Candida (grandchildren); Clara (mother); Lucio and Francisco Juahado (no relation given, but "works on farm" noted). This is the right family. We glean valuable information from this record. The three grandchildren were all born in Texas. Everyone else was born in Mexico. Petra and Clara are both marked as "widow." All of the family over the age of ten years, except Clara (age 80), has "works on farm" as their occupation. Lastly, we notice that some children are missing from the household: Porfiria, Jesus, Manuela, and Gregorio. What happened to these children?

We continue searching other sources. Because Petra is marked as "widow," we expect to find a marriage record for her before 1880. There is an index of Guadalupe county marriages available online, but you have to scan the list. Familysearch.org and Ancestry.com have searchable indexes. Our search returns a marriage record for Petra. Francisco Torres married Petra Ramires in 1874. The State Library in Austin maintains copies of Guadalupe county marriages on microfilm. Her marriage record includes a note showing that her father, Jesus Ramires, signed his permission for her to marry. This is the earliest record of the family living in Texas.

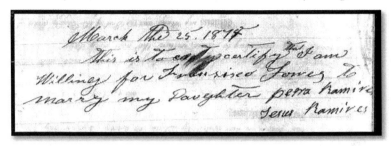

History Snapshot 4: This note was attached to the marriage record for Petra Ramirez and Francisco Guajardo; image courtesy of Lucinda Elizondo Anderson

Jesus' father, Jose Maria Ramirez, could have accompanied the family to Texas and died before 1880. That is also a possibility for Porfiria and Manuela. Clara, Jesus Ramirez's mother, is listed on the 1880 census, but not on the 1900. She presumably died between 1880 and 1900 in Texas.

Because most of the 1890 census (including records for Wilson and Guadalupe counties) was destroyed in a fire, we have no other information about Jesus and Jesusa as a family unit. Jesus died sometime before 1900. Jesusa is listed with her son, Jesus, and his family on the 1900 census and labeled as "widow." In 1910, she is listed with her granddaughter, Candida. The 1910 census recorded the year of immigration. For some of the family, that date is blank. Jesusa lists 1870 as the year of immigration, Austacio lists 1875, and Jesus and Ignacio both list 1872.

Family notes recorded Jesusa's death year as 1915 or 1916, but she is mentioned in her son's will in 1918 which he signed in April 1918. Jesus' will specified that $25 "shall be held in trust...and shall be paid toward her funeral expenses at her death." All other searches provide us no more information.

Oral History: Protestant

My mom grew up Methodist. Her mom was Methodist, her grandmother was Methodist, and her great grandfather was Methodist. Many descendants of Jesus and Jesusa relate the same story — Protestant grandparents and great grandparents.

We are not sure when or how so many in the family became Protestant. One story tells that the family was originally Catholic, but they left the Catholic church after someone was ill and the priest was too busy (or not willing) to visit the home.

Others talked about how the Methodist ministers would visit with the field workers and made travel to rural areas part of their regular circuit and many families were converted during these visits.

Going through family pictures, we found a picture of a Methodist church congregation in Chicago, IL taken in 1942. After much searching, several people were identified in the photo, and a branch of the family was discovered. Austacio's daughter and family were the Methodists in the Chicago congregation. One of Petra's daughters was Pentecostal, another daughter's family was Methodist, and others were Baptist. There is a thread that runs through this family: many are Protestant.

Much of the family that lived in Seguin, Texas, attended La Trinidad Iglesia Metodista (La Trinidad Methodist Church). David Maldonado, Jr., a great grandson of Petra Ramirez Suttles, wrote about that church in his book. *Crossing Guadalupe Street* is about growing up Protestant in a small Texas town.

Jesusa's children married and began having families of their own. They stayed in the Seguin area for several years. Jesusa's sons used to sit outside in the evenings speaking to each other in their "native tongue" – not Spanish. Whatever they were discussing, they didn't want to be overheard. Were they discussing political events in Mexico?

We know that the family that came up from Mexico, spoke a "native tongue" and were of Indian (and *mestizo*[10]) heritage. We don't know the language they spoke or the tribe from which they descended.

However, I heard from family (two people who had never met or spoken with each other) that their grandfathers recounted family stories and referred to the family as Apache. One told a story of his Apache grandmother. That story is recounted in Chapter 7: Petra.

About 1915, some families moved away in search of work to Houston, Dallas, Brownsville, New Orleans, and parts unknown. In the following chapters, you can read about the lives of Jesusa's children.

One descendant shared with me some old photos that were not labeled. She was pretty sure that they were from this family because of the other pictures that were with them. They are very old. They likely date to the time that the family all lived in Seguin, Texas. Who are they?

---

[10] Mestizo refers to people of mixed-race, especially Europeon and Native American

History Snapshot 5: Unknown Woman - Could this be Jesusa? Her clothing looks very native and unlike many other dresses in photos from this time period; photo courtesy of Abe Ramirez and Sarah Laffoday

History Snapshot 6: Unknown Man and child; It is obviously an old picture, but who is it? photo courtesy of Abe Ramirez and Sarah Laffoday

History Snapshot 7: Julian (Eliseo) Ramirez on the far right, Austacio next to him (we think), and two unknown men; photo courtesy of Abe Ramirez and Sarah Laffoday

4

Porfiria, (1849 – before 1880)

My uncle, Oscar Ramirez, Jr., spent many hours scrolling through microfilm and searching online. He found many of the christening records and showed me where to look online for records. FamilySearch.org is a great resource for researching ancestors in Texas and Mexico, and it's free!

To find all the children of Jesus and Jesusa, we can search using only the parents' names. We can also narrow the search by location to limit the results. In our results, the earliest christening record that lists Jesus Ramires as the father and Maria de Jesus Perales as the mother is for a Porfiria.

Porfiria Ramires was christened on 22 Sep 1849 in San Pablo, Galeana, Nuevo León, Mexico, by Tomas Garza Morales, the same priest that christened her mother 19 years before.

We know that Porfiria is not listed with her family in the 1880 census. Did she marry before that census? Did she die before 1880? We search Catholic and civil records in Mexico for a marriage or death record, but we find no records for her.

Maybe she came to Texas with her family and married before 1880. A search of marriages in Texas returns no marriage record for Porfiria. Because death records were not required until 1903, we surmise that she might have come to Texas but died before 1880.

5

Maria de San Juan, (1851 – 1852)

Searching through burial records one page at a time pays off when a death record for Maria de San Juan is found. Names in that record answer some questions and help take the tree back a few generations.

Maria de San Juan Ramires was christened in San Pablo on 22 Jan 1851. On the christening record, her parents are listed as Jesus Ramires and Maria de Jesus Perales.

Because Maria de San Juan is not listed on the 1880 census with her family, we search the death records in the San Pablo parish page by page, hoping to discover her fate. We find a death record for her.

She died of a fever on 7 Mar 1852 at the age of 14 months. Her burial record confirms that Jesus Ramires and Jose Cipriano de Jesus Alejandro are indeed the same person. Although she was christened as a daughter of Jesus Ramires, her burial record lists her parents' names as Jose de Jesus Alejandro and Maria de Jesus Perales. This is the only record we find recorded after their marriage in 1848 that uses the name Alejandro.

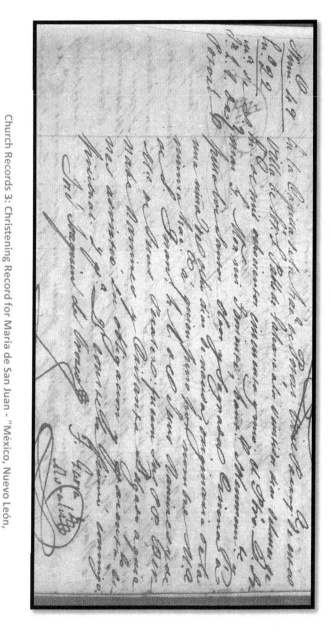

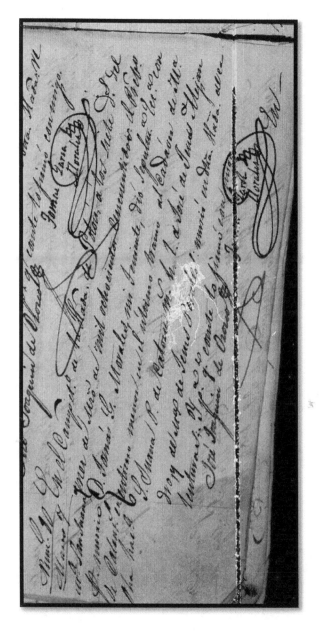

Church Records 4: Burial Record for Maria de San Juan - "México, Nuevo León, registros parroquiales, 1667-1981," images, FamilySearch (https://familysearch.org/pal:/MM9.3.1/TH-1-159380-102907-4?cc=1473204&wc=MCMK-K3F:453893014,53893024,46272401 : accessed 25 February 2015), Galeana > San Pablo > Defunciones 1851-1900 > image 80 of 457; Parroquias de la Iglesia Católica, Nuevo León [Catholic Church parishes, Nuevo León].

6

Jesus, (1853 – 1918)

The first bits of information known and gathered about Jesus Ramirez are credited to Herlinda Castañon Ramirez, his granddaughter. She was a keeper of family history. I have such fond memories of my Aunt Linda and am full of gratitude that she wrote down information and passed down stories.

History Snapshot 8: Herlinda Castañon Ramirez

Another source of the information about Jesus Ramirez is his great granddaughter, Gloria Munguia. She heard many stories and facts from her father that she passed on to me. My Uncle Oscar was a huge help in this process, as well. Without his research suggestions, guidance, and hundreds of exchanged emails, this could not have been written.

Our search using parents' names lists a Jesus Maria Ramires christened in El Potosí in the parish of San Pablo, Galeana, Nuevo León, Mexico, on 3 Jun 1853 at 6 days of age. He was between five and seven years old when he and his family moved from El Potosí to Saltillo.

The family moved to Texas when he was 19 years old. One story recounted to me was that young men were being prohibited from leaving Mexico in the 1870s. While I found no reference to this in the history books, I did find that military service was required for every male, but a waiver could be purchased. There is no record of the young Jesus ever serving in the military, and perhaps they did not have money for a waiver. As the story goes, Jesus, a young man of 19, dressed as a girl and sat in the wagon with his sisters, mother, and grandmother in order to get safely across the border. His brothers were young enough (8 & under) that they crossed without issue.

Jesus is not listed in his parents' household in the 1880 census. Is it possible that he married before that? He didn't die before 1880, because I know he lived long enough to father my great grandmother in 1882. A search of marriage records returns a result.

Jesus Ramirez married Urbana Ramos on 6 Jun 1875 in Comal County, Texas. She was about 14 years, and he was 22. It was unusual, but not unheard of for girls to marry so young. A list of their children is pieced together from census records, death records, and family notes. Jesus and Urbana had 13 children: Ramon, Leandro, Leonor, Dolores, David, Sara, Guadalupe, Plutarco, Josue, Guillermo, Anita, Clara, Carlos (see sections in this chapter).

Jesus is listed with his wife and children on the 1880 census; they are listed in Wilson County, Texas, – a county adjacent to Guadalupe County. Jesus' occupation was "shoemaker." Ramon,

Leandro, and Leonor are listed in the household with Jesus and Urbana.

The 1900 census lists Jesus, Urbana and family in Guadalupe County, Texas. His mother, Jesusa; his sister, Josefa; and his nephew, Alcario Torres (a son of Petra), are all listed in his household. No one is marked as "able to read or write," but later census records we find are marked differently. However, all of them, except his mother and sister, speak English. At age 47, Jesus is no longer working as a shoemaker. He is working on a rented farm, possibly as a sharecropper or tenant farmer for Willie Bentnagel or Louis Raul, landowners, who are listed above Jesus' household on the census.

Oral History: The Mystery of Urbana's Death

According to family, Urbana died in 1901. Strangely, Urbana is listed on the 1910 census; it states that she was born in Texas, had 12 children, and 8 were still alive. Norma Ramirez Banks remembered Aunt Linda talking about how Urbana died before Dolores' wedding in 1906.

In a box of papers at my Aunt Linda's house, we saw a wedding announcement for Dolores and Lamberto, Jr. The wedding was announced only by her father Jesus Ramirez.

On the 1910 census, Jesus is listed as an employee on a General Farm. Urbana is listed on the census, although family accounts say that she died in 1901 (or at least before 1906). Jesus and his children are marked as "able to read and write."

Sometime after arriving in Texas, Jesus converted from Catholicism to Methodism. I was told that he worked with other men in the community to build a Spanish-speaking Methodist church in Seguin, Texas. Some of his children, grandchildren, and great grandchildren were active in that church– *La Trinidad Iglesia Metodista* (La Trinidad Methodist Church). The church is still meeting every Sunday at 306 E Gonzales in Seguin, Texas.

Jesus was born into poverty in a small village in Mexico, journeyed miles to a new home as a child, and again as a young adult. While his life in Texas was simple, he built a life that left a legacy. In his will, he left land, goods, and monies to his family. The

History Snapshot 10: (back row) Sara, David, Dolores, Leandro, Leonor, Ramon, Plutarco (front row) Guillermo, Jesus Ramirez, Anita, Urbana Ramos, Carlos (in her lap), and Josue; photo taken about 1901; from my Aunt Linda's photos

photo of his family (taken about 1901) shows a neatly dressed family all wearing shoes. Did he make those shoes?

Finding Jesus' death certificate, we discover that he died on 9 July 1918 after a long battle with tuberculosis and was buried in Riverside Cemetery in Seguin, Texas. We do not know where Urbana is buried, but Rodolfo, a grandson of Jesus, told his daughter, Gloria Munguia, that Urbana was buried in Riverside cemetery in the family plot.

Gloria Munguia remembered her father taking her to Riverside cemetery and showing her where his grandfather was buried. The grave was marked with a cross. We believe this broken cross is his headstone. It sits in the shade of a tree in Riverside Cemetery (Sec 13 Plot 6).

History Snapshot 11: Jesus Ramirez's Grave

A Note about tuberculosis: There are many people throughout this family's history that suffered from or died of tuberculosis. Tuberculosis (TB), also known as consumption, is an infectious disease that typically affects the lungs. It is spread through coughs and sneezes. In some places, there were sanatoriums set up for people with TB to be isolated and try to recover. Other times, people stayed in their own homes and tried to limit contact as much as possible. People with TB would often suffer a long, agonizing illness, withering away and eventually being unable to breathe. Until the wide-spread use of antibiotics during World War II, there was no treatment for tuberculosis.

Ramon Ramirez

We pieced together a list of children, and we know that Ramon Ramirez is the oldest son of Jesus and Urbana. His death certificate lists his birth date as 31 Aug 1876. His christening record, found in the Catholic Archives in San Antonio, lists his birth date as 30 June 1876 and his christening date as 14 Oct 1876. He is listed on the 1880 and 1900 censuses with Jesus and Urbana. Browsing the Guadalupe County marriage index, we find a marriage entry for Ramon Ramirez and Matilde Antu on 20 Nov 1902. A trip to the Guadalupe Courthouse in Seguin, Texas, or the State Library in Austin, Texas, lets us see a copy of the actual certificate.

They had five children (see list at the end of this section). In the 1910 census, they are listed in Guadalupe County, very near his father's household. Ramon is living on a farm working "on his own account."

After only 18 years of marriage, Matilde died on 1 Jun 1920 from kidney failure. Her death certificate lists her only as Mrs. Ramon Ramirez. She was buried in Riverside Cemetery in Seguin, Texas.

Oral History: Ramon Ramirez

Ramon was described to me by three of his granddaughters: Ninfa Garcia, Dora Rodriguez, and Tillie Guitierrez. He was an eloquent speaker that was often asked to speak at the Deis y Seis de Septiembre and other gatherings in Seguin. He enjoyed writing poetry, and sometimes it was read on the radio. "A very disciplined man" who taught his granddaughter how to read and write in Spanish using the Bible. He was a man of strong Methodist faith.

Ramon's granddaughters mentioned that Ramon used to write poetry. Gloria Munguia sent me a poem written by Ramon. The English translation is included in the End Notes.

A mi madre: Matilde A. Ramírez (by Ramón Ramírez)*

Madres, Madre, nombre, nombre sagrado,
Que Cristo con sus labios pronunció.

Hoy aquí te pronuncio yo.
Porque de Dios el amor no igualado
Sólo a ti fue doble participar.
Por eso esta noche delante del altar de este humilde
Y sagrado resinto, con todo respeto
Mi rodilla hinco, al decir "madre,"
Y tu amor reverencia, ya no te
Miro a mi lado estar, ni de tus
Labios recibo la dulce ternura,
Pero si, con mi inocensia pura,
¡Te veo en Angélico Lugar!

Quién no se siente dichoso
Al contemplar la imagen de su
Madre en cuyos labios no hay fingido
Alarde, en cuyo corazón no hay
Sentimiento vanidoso, Yo por eso
Mucho envidio a los que todav¡a
Tienen ese privilegio,
Pues es un tesoro en su provecho
Que yo desde mi infancia he perdido.

Aprovechar pues ese galardón
Los que todavía teneís a vuestra madre
Mientras esa dicha no se acabe
Gosareís de grande satisfacción
Amarla con todo el corazón
Y de sus consejos andar en pos
Verla siempre con veneración
Pues así lo manda Dios.
Niños este día a la madre dedicado
Nos dé una idea muy definida
A ese hacer de amor privilegiado
Que sea para nosotros lección de agrado
Y más impulse nuestra obedencia.

In 1925, Ramon married Margarita Gallegos. She had children from a previous marriage, but they had no children together. Margarita died in 1947 and was buried in Riverside Cemetery.

Ramon purchased an entire block on Ireland Street in Seguin, Texas. He lived in the house at 521 E Ireland and his children built other houses down the block. He was active up to the very end. His granddaughter told me that in 1964 Ramon was kicked in the head by a mule and died of a brain aneurism soon after. He died 13 Mar 1964 at 87 years of age and was buried in Riverside Cemetery in Seguin, Texas. Viewing the image of the death certificate, we see that Ramon is listed as a retired farmer. There is information on the actual death certificate that is not indexed, such as the date of burial, the informant's name, the cause of death, and sometimes a last known street address.

History Snapshot 12: (left) Ramon Ramirez; (right) Ramon Ramirez with his grandchild; photos courtesy of Ninfa Garcia and Dora Rodriguez

Children of Ramon and Matilde:

1. Daniel (1904 – 1958) married Rosa Hurtado (1902 - 1977)
2. Jesus (1905 – 1926) never married
3. Sara (1908 – 1937) married Jose Sosa
4. Juanita (1912 – 2003) married Fernando Zambrano (1913 – 1993)
5. Elvira (1918 – 1994) married Catarino Carmona (1921 - 1992)

All five children stayed in the Seguin area until their death. Daniel and his wife, Rosa, are buried in St James Cemetery in Seguin, Texas. Jesus; Sara and her young son, Jose Jr; Juanita and her husband, Fernando; and Elvira and her husband, Catarino are all buried in Riverside cemetery. There are markers in the Ramirez Family Plot (Section 13 – Plots 6 &9) for Jesus, Juanita, Fernando, Elvira, and Catarino. Riverside is noted as the location of burial for Sara Sosa and Jose Jr., but there are no legible headstones for them in the family plot.

Leandro Ramirez

Leandro Ramirez was born on 13 Mar 1877. He is listed on the 1880 and 1900 censuses with his parents. On 21 Jan 1907 he married Maria Alfaro[11] in Guadalupe County, Texas. They had four children (see list on next page). In the 1910 census they are listed in Guadalupe County, near Leandro's uncle, Austacio Ramirez. A daughter, Carolina, and two other children are listed on the 1910 census, but Carolina is not listed on the 1920 census. Presumably she died sometime between 1910 and 1920. No death record for her was found.

We have a difficult time finding his death certificate because his name is spelled Leander Ramerez and his parents names are badly misspelled. Searching his first name and the county of death, results in a list that contains his death certificate. Leandro died on 4 May 1912 at age 35 from a gunshot wound. It was whispered that his wound was self-inflicted. His death certificate only lists Seguin, Texas, as the place of burial.

In the 1920 census, Maria and children are listed with her parents, Fidencio & Florencia Alfaro, in Guadalupe County. She and the children are still listed with them in the 1930 census, but in San Antonio. Maria died on 29 Aug 1934 and is buried in San Jose Burial Park in San Antonio, Texas, very near her parents' graves.

---

[11] Additional notes: Maria's sister, Carlota Alfaro, married Delfino Ramos, a brother of Urbana (wife of Jesus.) Isabel Alfaro, Maria's aunt, married Austacio Ramirez (a brother of Jesus.)

Children of Leandro and Maria:

1. Clara (1908 – 1985) married Abraham Ibarra (1903 - 1984)
2. Carolina (1909 - ?) death likely before 1920
3. Gilberto (1909 - 1990) married Leonor Barbosa (1909 -)
4. Alonzo (1911 – 1995) married Cristina Cuevas (1914 - 1952)

Clara, Gilberto, and Alonzo were very young when their father died and only in their twenties when their mom passed away. According to Alonzo's daughter, they received a lot of help from their Alfaro aunts who also lived in San Antonio. All three children stayed in San Antonio until their deaths.

Oral History: Clarita & Ninfa Ibarra

Norma Ramirez Banks, my mom, remembered sitting on her grandmother's porch when visitors came to see Dolores "Lola" Castañon in her last days. My mom remembered the names Clarita and Ninfa and the last name Ibarra. Clarita Ramirez Ibarra, Dolores' niece, and Clarita's daughter, Ninfa, would visit Lola when she was sick.

My mom also remembers Leonor Muniz visiting her grandma. Leonor was Maria Alfaro Ramirez's sister. She was one of the Alfaro aunts mentioned above.

Leonor Ramirez Sarabia

Leonor was born on 21 Feb 1880 according to her christening record. She was christened on 10 Apr 1880 at the Catholic Church in St. Hedwig, St. Mary of the Annunciation. She is listed with Jesus and Urbana on the 1900 census. On 7 Nov 1906 she married Santiago Sarabia. They had five children (see list on next page). At age 34, Leonor died of tuberculosis on 14 Apr 1915. A contributory cause of death is noted as "No Doctor." Her death certificate only lists Seguin, Texas, as the burial location. It is possible that she was buried in Riverside Cemetery like so many others in the family.

Children of Leonor and Santiago:

1. Celia (1908 - 1999) married Zaragosa "Gus" Maldonado[12] (1907 - 2001)
2. Jesus (1911 – 1914)
3. Margerita (1913 – 1913)
4. Jose (1914 – 1914)
5. Ernesto (died in infancy)

Sadly, Celia was the only child to live beyond childhood. After her mother's death she lived in the Beeville, Texas, area with her dad. Celia and her husband, Gus Maldonado, stayed in the Beeville area until their deaths.

Dolores Ramirez Castañon

Dolores was born on 19 Feb 1882 near Seguin, Texas, and christened in the Catholic Church in St Hedwig, Texas, (a nearby town) on 16 April 1882. She is listed on the 1900 census with her parents. On 13 Dec 1906, she married Lamberto Castañon, Jr. in Guadalupe County. They had nine children (see list at the end of this section).

On the 1910 census, Lamberto, Jr and Dolores are listed in Guadalupe County next to his parents and family. They were working on the farm of Willie Bauer. In the 1920 census, they are still listed in Guadalupe County on New Braunfels Road. From family stories, I believe they were still working as sharecroppers or tenant farmers for Willie Bauer. I am not sure what crops they were growing, but historical accounts of the area all mention cotton as a

---

[12] Additional note: Gus Maldonado was a cousin of Samuel Maldonado that married Emma Suttles.

major crop in that area. They were likely planting, growing, and picking cotton.

History Snapshot 13: (left) Dolores Ramirez (right) Dolores and Lamberto Castañon, Jr on their wedding day; from my Aunt Linda's photos

Oral History: Memories of the Farm

My grandma, Herminia Castañon Ramirez would sometimes share memories about living on the farm, before they moved to San Antonio. My mom remembered her talking about when her younger brother was about to be born. All the children went to stay with a neighbor, a black family that lived nearby on the farm.

My grandma spoke fondly of Willie Bauer, almost as if he were family. Willie Bauer was the landowner on whose land they did sharecropping or tenant farming. There is a recipe for a meat dressing that she made every

Thanksgiving. She'd gotten the recipe from the Bauer family. My aunt, Yolanda Ramirez Flores, sent me the recipe. She had the ingredients list that my grandma wrote down, but she helped fill 'in the blanks by adding the instructions.

Ground Meat
1 or 2 Potatoes
Raisins
Pecans or Almonds
Cloves
Sugar
Very little salt
1-2 Slices of bread

(1) Cook the ground meat. (2) Just before the meat is completely cooked, add the 1 or 2 cubed potatoes and finish cooking meat and potatoes. (3) Add 1 or 2 slices of toasted bread cut into small pieces. (4) Add raisins and pecans (or almonds). If you add almonds, boil them slightly and cool so that you can peel them easily and then chop the almonds or sliver them and add to the dressing.(5) Add sugar, cloves spice, and a little salt to the meat mixture. Simmer the dressing until all the flavors mellow.

About 1922, Lamberto, Dolores and family packed up their belongings and moved to San Antonio. Their first house in San Antonio was at 849 Delgado. Then they bought the house at 2303 Arbor Place, where they lived out the rest of their days.

Dolores and her husband always had a garden; it seems Lamberto, Jr. could never shake his farming instincts. He was part of the 100 man WPA crew that renovated and expanded the San Antonio Zoo. I was told that he worked on the additions to Monkey Island (which was done away with in more recent renovations). Then later, Lamberto, Jr worked as a janitor for the San Antonio public schools and as a groundskeeper for the principal, Ms. Banks.[13]

Oral History: The family on Arbor Place

Many of Dolores' and Lamberto's children lived on or near Arbor Place.

- Their daughter, Linda, and her husband, Isidro, lived at 2302 Arbor Place
- Their son, Lambert, and his wife, Susie, lived at 2222 Arbor Place
- Their son, Tembo (Artemio), and his wife, Kate, lived at 2203 Arbor Place
- Their daughter, Mina (my grandma), and her husband, Oscar (my grandpa), lived at 2107 Arbor Place
- Their son, Leo, and his wife, Susie, lived 4 or 5 blocks away on Ruiz, on the other side of Ogden Elementary school
- Their son, Joe, and his wife, Henrietta, later moved to Goodrich Ave, just 8 or 9 blocks away

Fourteen cousins attended Ira Ogden Elementary School, many of them all at one time!

Dolores and Lamberto were known for loaning money to family as long as it was paid back at the end of each month. Dolores kept a ledger of the accounts. She had good bookkeeping skills.

During the depression, Dolores and her daughters helped earn money for the household by making baby clothes. One person would sew, one would do embroidery, and another the smocking, etc. Each had their own job in the process. Dolores' granddaughters remember how she would lay out the newspaper and cut a pattern

---

[13] Ms. Banks was not related to my dad, Daniel Banks.

for whatever dress she wanted to make. She even made some dresses out of organza.

Dolores attended La Trinidad Methodist Church in San Antonio. Lamberto did not attend church with her, but every Sunday he would take Dolores, go by and pick up my grandma and her kids and drive them all to church. My mom remembers that when her grandpa picked them up after church, he'd have hot corn tortillas in the car for them.

Dolores died on 13 Jan 1956 after a battle with colon cancer. Lamberto lived another ten years after her death. Shortly before his death he moved to a nursing home. While there, in his last few days of his life, he would tell the staff that he could see his wife picking flowers outside his window. He died on 4 Oct 1966 at age 80. They are buried side by side in San Jose Burial Park in San Antonio, Texas.

Children of Dolores and Lamberto, Jr:

1. Leopoldo (1907 - 1989) married Susie Herrera (1909 - 2004)
2. Gilbert (1909 - 1936) married Teresa Najera (1908 -2012)
3. Jose "Joe"(1910 - 1989) married Enriqueta de la Cruz (1913 - 2005)
4. Herminia "Mina" (1911-1986) married Oscar Ramirez[14] (1915-1992)
5. Virginia (1913 – 2003) married Henry Sanchez (1908 - 1998)
6. Herlinda "Linda" (1914-1991) married Isidro Ramirez[14] (1916-1981)
7. Armando "Mando"(1918-1997) married Ellen Hohenberger (1914-2005)
8. Lamberto "Lambert"(1920-2005) married Susie Rodriguez (1922-2011)
9. Artemio "Tembo"(1923-2002) married Katherine Vallejo (1925 -)

All the children, except Leopoldo, lived out their lives in San Antonio. In their later years, Leopoldo and Susie moved to California to be near one of their sons. They both died in California.

---

[14] Oscar and Isidro were brothers. They were not related to the Ramirez family that came from El Potosí.

History Snapshot 14: Armando, Herlinda, Leopoldo, Lamberto Castañon Jr., Dolores Ramirez Castañon holding Rose Marie (daughter of Virginia), Joe, Virginia, Herminia, Artemio, and Lamberto. This photo was taken in Seguin in 1938.

History Snapshot 15: Gilbert Castañon Sr. Gilbert is not in the picture above because he died of tuberculosis in Feb 1936; photo courtesy of Michelle Perez

David Ramirez

David was born on 5 Sep 1884. He is listed on the 1900 census with his parents; his occupation is listed as "farmer." He died on 28 May 1910 at age 25 of pneumonia. He was buried in Riverside Cemetery in Seguin, Texas.

Sara Ramirez

Sara was born in Jan 1887 according to the 1900 census. There is a picture of the family taken about 1901 (late in that year probably) and she is listed as in the photo. Our other searches turn up no other information about Sara.

Guadalupe Ramirez

Guadalupe is listed in Aunt Linda's notes, but there are no other records for Guadalupe. We don't even know if Guadalupe was male or female. Guadalupe is not listed on the 1900 census and is not listed in the family photo taken about 1901.

Plutarco Ramirez

Plutarco was born on 25 Nov 1890 in Guadalupe County. He is listed in his father's household in the 1900 and 1910 censuses. He married Elvira Escobeda on 5 Jan 1911. Elvira died in 1912 at age 18. They had one child that died in infancy.

On 6 Aug 1914, Plutarco married Isabel Rivera in Seguin, Texas. They had 11 children (see list on the next page). Plutarco was a sharecropper; he and his family moved to Petronila in Nueces County to clear the land and run the farm for the land owner they'd worked for in the Seguin area. This landowner was very good to Plutarco, almost more of a friend than a boss.

Isabel died on 15 Sep 1968 at age 72. Plutarco followed soon after on 27 Nov 1968. They were both buried in Seaside Memorial Park in Corpus Christi, Texas.

Children of Plutarco and Isabel:

1. Rodolfo (1915 – 1986) married Carolina Medina (1918 – 2014)
2. Elisa (1918 – 2006) married Manuel Saucedo
3. Altagracia (1919 – 1999) married Henry Ruiz
4. Marcial (1921 – 2002) married Ofelia Saenz
5. Oralia (1923 -)
6. Jesus "Chuy" (1927 – 1953)
7. Ernesto (1928 -)
8. Delia (1929 – 1929)
9. Rogelio (1931 -) married Olga De Leon
10. Alfredo (1932 -) married Norma Perez
11. Plutarco Jr (1934 -) married Esther Serna

History Snapshot 16: Plutarco and Isabel Ramirez with their granddaughter, Viola Ramirez; photo courtesy of Viola Ramirez Gutierrez

History Snapshot 17: Plutarco Ramirez and his son, Rodolfo Ramirez; photo courtesy of Gloria Munguia

Oral History: Uncle Chuy's Death

By Gloria Munguia

Uncle Chuy returned from the Korean War to his home in Corpus Christi with dreams of owning a car, building a house, getting married and having children. He had saved most of his money while in Korea so he wasted no time buying a car. Next he purchased a lot in a very nice subdivision of town where emerging Mexican-Americans were building their dream homes. But Uncle Chuy also had a bad habit. He liked to drink.

One particular weekend he and friend Juan drove to Laredo for some fun across the Mexican border. Of course, drinking was on the agenda. On their return trip to Corpus

Christi, Uncle Chuy stepped on the accelerator driving faster and faster on the lonely road where one could go for miles without meeting another vehicle. He liked the cool night air slapping his face bringing a little relief to his drunken self. Juan begged Uncle Chuy to slow down, but Uncle Chuy, just back from the Korean War, felt invincible. He was back in America. What could go wrong? Things went wrong very quickly as he lost control of the car rolling over three times. Juan remembers glancing at Uncle Chuy as he pulled his head out through the opened door which quickly closed slamming on Uncle Chuy's temples. He was killed instantly.

Around the same time, over a hundred miles away, my parents [Rodolfo and Carolina Ramirez] slept in their farm home with all of the windows opened allowing the breeze to cool the house. Suddenly they were aroused from their sleep by the sounds of metal crashing and wheels screeching. They both simultaneously sat up and asked each other, What was that? Surely a car had crashed. Grabbing a flashlight, my father walked outside. He could see nothing on the road. He shone the flashlight across the acres of land and again nothing. Strange, he thought. Both he and Mother had heard a crash; yet there was no evidence of an accident. Puzzled, they both returned to their bed and fell asleep again.

Morning arrived. Again my father went out looking for signs of an accident. Finding none, he returned to the house where he and my mother continued with their morning coffee. Shortly after, the neighbor who had the only telephone for miles around arrived with the tragic news of Uncle Chuy's death. Stunned, my father walked into the house and announced the death of his brother to my mother. They stood in the kitchen trying not to believe what they had just heard. In their sorrow, they recalled the sounds of the crash just a few hours earlier. Could that have been Uncle Chuy's ghost traversing the miles to come say good-bye to his oldest brother?

History Snapshot 18: Uncle Chuy; photo courtesy of Gloria Munguia

Josue Ramirez

Dates and information on a death certificate are provided by an informant, usually a family member, and sometimes the information is not correct. Josue's death certificate lists his birth date as 18 Mar 1903, but since he is listed on the 1900 census living with his parents, it seems the date might be wrong. More searching helps us find his World War I Draft Registration Card. That lists his birth date as 18 Mar 1893. That seems right. He is listed in his father's household in the 1910 census also. Sometime before June 1917, he married Trinidad Garcia. They had three children: Cimitrio, Hortencia and another sister whose name we haven't found. (see list at the end of this section)

History Snapshot 19: Josue, Cimitrio, and Hortencia (we think); photo courtesy of Sergio Ramirez

Sadly, Trinidad died on 30 Apr 1922 after a two-month battle with tuberculosis. She was buried in Riverside Cemetery in Seguin, Texas. Hortencia died of food poisoning on 2 Aug 1925 in Seguin, Texas. Sometime after Trinidad's death, Cimitrio went to live with his uncle, Vidal Garcia, in San Diego, Texas. At first we only knew about Cimitrio, but the photo of Josue with two children spurs another search and we uncover birth and death information for Hortencia. Interestingly, Cimitrio's son recently learned from someone else that grew up in Uncle Vidal's home that Cimitrio had two full sisters. No documentation is found about the other sister.

About 1925, Josue married Petra Ramirez (no relation). Josue and Petra settled in the Robstown area and had six children (see list on next page). Josue was a farm worker.

He died on 17 Jul 1968 of pneumonia; Parkinson's disease is listed as a contributing cause. He had Parkinson's for 10 years. He was buried in Robstown Memorial Park.

Child of Josue and Trinidad Garcia:

1. Cimitrio (1918 – 1981) married Aurora Garcia (1919 - 2012)
2. Hortencia (1920-1925)
3. Unknown daughter

Children of Josue and Petra Ramirez:

4. Leonor (1926 -) married Sam Leal (1921-2001)
5. Josue (1928 – 2000) married Hilda Franco
6. Minerva (1930 -) married Enrique Garcia
7. Beatrice (1936 -) married Eleasar Vasquez
8. Filiberto (1937 -) married Maria Elena Garza
9. Ramon (1939 -)

Oral History: Memories of my dad, Cimitrio
By Ricardo Ramirez

My dad often visited with his brother, Joe, and was very proud of his brother, Ramon, who went on to get higher education degrees. According to Ramon's wife, my dad was always there to give Ramon encouragement and support in his early years of getting an education. Dad valued an education as a way to get ahead in life. He did not want me to experience the struggles he encountered in his life and this [education] was the way to avoid it.

My dad was very close to the man that took him in, Tío Vidal or Papa Vidal as I called him. Dad worked at his service station as long as I can remember as his manager/bookkeeper during the week and on weekends we would help out at the ranch. My dad did everything he could for Vidal. I guess he was just trying to pay him back for everything he did for him while growing up.

My dad was a family man always providing for my mother and me first. My dad was strict and never spoiled me but he also never left me to want anything. He also had a kind heart always willing to help anyone in need.

Guillermo Ramirez

Guillermo was born on 17 Feb 1895. He is listed in his father's household on the 1900 and 1910 censuses. He married Estefana Zepeda. They settled in the Houston area and had eight children. (see list on the next page)

History Snapshot 20: Guillermo and Estefana on their wedding day

According to his death certificate, Guillermo served in World War I. He died on 18 Apr 1955 in Houston, Texas. He was buried in Forest Park Cemetery. Estefana died in 1987 in Houston, Texas.

History Snapshot 21: (back row) Armando, Ninfa, Rosalie (wife of Leandro), Leandro, Josie, Willie Jr, Anita; (front row) Ramiro, Estefana Zepeda Ramirez, Gilbert, Vincente, Guillermo Ramirez, Margaret; photo courtesy of Yolanda Garza

Children of Guillermo and Estefana:

1. Ninfa (1921 –) married Gilbert Sarabia
2. Liandro (1923 - 2007) married Rosalie Palacios
3. Josie (1925 –) married Nate Torres
4. Guillermo Jr (1926 – 1973) married Sara Escamilla
5. Anita (1928 – 2000) married Albert Gonzales
6. Armando (1930 – 1968) married Cruz Zapata
7. Vicente (1932 – 2004) married Ruth Falcon (1933 – 1982) after Ruth's death married Mary Morin, but they had no children
8. Ramiro (1934 –) married Angela Alvarez
9. Margaret Elida (1936 –) married Berton F "Mike" Hughes
10. Leopoldo Gilbert (1939 –) married Linda Romo

Anita Ramirez Briones

A search for "Anita" entering "Jesus Ramirez" as the father and a birthplace of "Seguin, TX", returns census records and a death certificate on familysearch.org. From her death certificate we learn her married name and her birth date. Anita was born on 6 Jan 1897, and we know she married a Briones. She is listed in her father's household on the 1900 and 1910 censuses. She married Reyes Briones and they had one son, Ernesto Briones. Sadly, Anita died on 29 Jul 1922 from tuberculosis; she was only 25 years old. She was buried in Riverside Cemetery in Seguin, Texas. After her death, Reyes Briones and his son, Ernesto, moved to Corpus Christi, TX. Reyes remarried, had other children, and lived in Corpus Christi until his death in 1988.

Child of Anita and Ernesto:

1. Ernesto (1920 – 2004) married Amelia Aleman

Clara Ramirez

The 1900 census lists a Clara in the household, born in Feb 1899. She is not in the family photo taken about 1901.

Oral History: Losing a sister

Herlinda Castañon Ramirez spoke of how her mother, Dolores, handled Urbana's death. Dolores lost a sister sometime before her mother died and grieved very deeply for her sister - was saddened to the point of depression. She was better able to handle her mother's death because she had already dealt with the death of her sister. Perhaps this account refers to losing Clara or Guadalupe, who were both missing from the family photo in 1901.

Carlos Ramirez

The Social Security Death Index lists Carlos's birth date as 21 Feb 1901. He was the youngest son of Jesus and Urbana. His mother died the same year he was born. His older sisters helped to rear him. Carlos moved to New York City in 1928 and lived in that area until he returned to San Antonio about 1967 (except during his time in the military). His sister, Dolores, was hurt that he rarely came to see her, although he did visit shortly before her death in 1956. I was told that, while in New York, he worked at a cigar shop in a hotel lobby. Records show that he also served in the military during World War II.

When he returned to the San Antonio area, he lived in the rear apartment behind Aunt Linda's house on Arbor Place. Then he moved to the little house on the "Ranchito" in Helotes, Texas, when Herlinda & Isidro Ramirez moved out there. The "Ranchito" had a rear apartment and he lived there until not long before he died. He had Parkinson's disease and needed full-time nursing care so he moved to a nursing home shortly before his death. He died on 11 Jun 1988 in San Antonio, Texas, and was buried in Fort Sam Houston National Cemetery.

History Snapshot 22: Carlos Ramirez; photos courtesy of Ninfa Garcia and Dora Rodriguez

Oral History: Carlos Ramirez

Carlos loved to dance. Almost every weekend he went out dancing in New York. His grand nieces remembered seeing a picture of him all dressed up wearing a boutonnière. Working in the cigar shop, he met several gentlemen that worked on Wall Street. These repeat customers gave him investment tips and Carlos invested. This allowed him to save up a small bundle and "retire" in San Antonio. He also left money to each of his nephews and nieces when he died.

Rose De Hoyos visited him when he lived in New York. She remembered how frugally he lived. He had only two forks because he didn't need more than that.

Some of his great grand nieces and nephews remember that he gave them $1 each time he saw them.

Some people wondered why he never married. He was persnickety. He had a list; his sisters would shake their heads at him and tell him that with that list he would never marry. He never did. No one ever measured up.

7

Petra, (1856 – 1918)

Never underestimate the importance of a remembered first name! As I researched, I would call my mom to ask questions. During one conversation she remembered that her mom, Herminia Castañon Ramirez, would speak with a cousin, Tana, on the phone around Christmastime each year. She wanted to know how Tana was related. I found how Tana was related and also found an entire branch of the family – Petra's branch. One small piece of information can lead to a big find. A helpful research tool was my Aunt Linda's address book. It was a great place to start when I only had a first name.

We start with the address book, looking for a Tana. We know that is a nickname for Cayetana (or Calletana). We find an entry for Julio Castillo whose listing has a note in parentheses "Cayetana Rodriguez."

History Snapshot 23: Entry from Aunt Linda's Address Book

Searching census records for Tana Rodriguez, we find her mother's name, Candida. Then we search for Candida in the census. We find her living with her mother and grandparents in 1880. Her mother is Petra Ramirez and her grandparents are Jesus and Jesusa Ramirez. (This record, also mentioned in Chapter 3, is really what began my quest. From this record I learned that Jesus, my great great grandfather, had not come to Texas alone. He had come with his family.)

We know from our earlier searches of christening records that Petra was born on 29 May 1856 and christened on 4 Jun 1856 in El Potosí, part of the San Pablo parish in Galeana, Nuevo León, Mexico. She traveled with her family from El Potosí to Saltillo when she was two or three and then from Saltillo to Texas when she was 16 years old.

As mentioned earlier, Petra, age 17, married Francisco Torres on 13 Apr 1874 in Guadalupe County, Texas. He was quite a bit older than Petra according to her granddaughter-in-law. They had 3 children: Alcario, Samuel, and Candida (see sections in this chapter). Francisco died sometime before the 1880 census. Petra is listed as a widow in the 1880 census; she was only 24 years old.

The story of Francisco Torres' death was recounted to me by a great grandson of Petra. His grandfather was Petra's oldest son from her second marriage. Francisco Torres was riding his horse when a stranger, who seemed a bit off, asked for a ride. Francisco agreed to give him a ride and let him climb up behind him on the horse. Sometime during the ride, the stranger reached around and stabbed Francisco in the abdomen. He died from his injury.

Marriage records show that Petra married Francisco Guajardo, age 25, on 29 Oct 1880 in Guadalupe County (see Associated Families Chapter for more information about the Guajardo family). They had 3 children: Maria, Francisco Jr. and Elias (see sections in this chapter). Francisco Guajardo presumably died sometime before 1886.

Oral History: Guajardo brothers

In the 1880 census, there were two farm laborers boarding with the Jesus Ramirez family: Francisco Guajardo and Lucio Guajardo. Petra married Francisco Guajardo and Petra's sister, Estefana, married Lucio Guajardo. There is a family story that sisters married brothers. Perhaps these are to whom the story refers.

The Bexar County Clerk's Office has a searchable database that allows us to view past records. After finding an index entry for a Bexar County marriage for Petra, we look up the PDF file, a scan of the original marriage license. On 10 Oct 1886, Petra and Jasper (Gaspar) Suttles were married in Bexar County; her parents were witnesses at the ceremony. The marriage was performed by Elias Robertson, a minister of the Methodist Church.

They settled in the town of New Berlin and farmed there. They had 4 children: Jasper Jr. (Gaspar Jr.), Maria, Emma, and Edward (see sections in this chapter). Jasper Suttles was born in Mississippi according to census records. He was described as an Englishman who spoke Spanish with an English accent. (David Maldonado)

History Snapshot 24: Gaspar Suttles and Petra Ramirez Suttles; photos courtesy of Ernestine Andrada

After 31 years of marriage, Petra and Jasper died one day apart in 1918. Petra died on 11 Feb 1918 of pneumonia brought on by "La grippe," another word for influenza or flu. Jasper died on 12 Feb 1918 also from influenza, specifically the Spanish flu. They were both buried in Kuehler Catholic Cemetery in Guadalupe County which is now called Santa Clara Cemetery. Headstones were not found. Many headstones in the cemetery are illegible or broken.

Oral History: Apache Grandmother

One of the stories referring to the family as Apache was about Petra's death. A great, great granddaughter of Petra heard the story from her grandfather. Her grandfather told her about his Apache grandmother. When Petra lay sick and dying, she looked over to the bed beside her and told her husband, Gaspar, who was also very ill, that she was dying soon, but that after she died, she would come for him. Petra died on a Monday morning in Feb; Gaspar died twelve hours later, but his death was not recorded until the next day.

The pandemic "Spanish Flu" of 1918 claimed as many as 50 million lives worldwide. Several of our family members in the Seguin area were impacted by this flu. This flu mainly targeted healthy young adults who lacked any prior exposure; those who had exposure to similar flu strains had built up at least some immunity.

Alcario Torres

Alcario's death certificate lists his birth date as 12 Jan 1874. As mentioned earlier, dates on death certificates are provided by informants so they are not always correct. His parents married in March of 1874, so he may have been born in Jan of 1875. Alcario was described as tall, fair, and good-looking; but he never married. Alcario worked as a farm laborer.

Alcario died on 1 Aug 1946 in San Antonio after battling stomach cancer. His name is misspelled as "Arcadio Torrez" on his death certificate. He was buried in San Jose Burial Park.

Samuel Torres

There is a birth record for Samuel, born on 1 Apr 1877 in Graytown, Wilson County, Texas. He is listed on the 1880 census with his mother and grandparents, but no other records for him turn up in our searches.

Candida Torres Rodriguez

We know from the 1880 census that Candida was born about 1878. Her death certificate lists her birth date as 3 Oct 1878. She married Serapio Rodriguez in 1900, and they had nine children (see list on the next page).

Candida was mentioned by many different people with whom I spoke. She worked to maintain family connections and helped family whenever necessary. In 1910, her grandmother, Jesusa, and her aunt, Josefa, lived with her according to the census. When her younger brother, Elias, lost his wife to the Spanish flu, Candida took in his children.

Oral History: Candida Torres Rodriguez

Candida was described as a beautiful person to know. She kept in touch with family: nephews, nieces, and cousins. One person commented that her children, even after they'd moved out and had a family, were always at her house.

Another person mentioned that every single wall of her house was covered in pictures.

A niece remembered that when visiting, Candida would always give cookies to the children. She would do this every time they visited until she was sick and was no longer able to get up.

Her husband, Serapio, died on 29 Oct 1939 at age 76. Candida died on 31 Aug 1956 at age 77. Near the end of her life, she was wheelchair bound, but she had a sharp mind to the very end. They were both buried in Concrete Cemetery in Wilson County, Texas.

Children of Candida and Serapio:

1. Santos (1904 - 1975) married Angelita Vasquez (1919 - 2005)
2. Petra (1906 - 1942) married Pablo Elizondo (1902 - 1950)
3. Serapio (1908 - 1986) married Hilaria "LaLa" Vasquez
4. Calletana "Tana" (1907 - 1992) married Julio Castillo (1912 - 2003)
5. Adelina (1910 - 1980) married Andres Almazan (1911 - 1985)
6. Martina (1912 - 1980) married Cecil John Ruiz (1912 - 1981)
   married Dalton Crates (1910- 1996)
7. Candida (1914 -) married Julian Garcia
8. Abram (abt 1917 - ?) died young
9. Consuelo (1920 – 1951) married Celestino Cervantes

History Snapshot 25: Serapio and Candida with their granddaughter, Esperanza, and unknown baby. Tragically, Esperanza "Hope" was murdered when she was only in her teens; photo courtesy of Mary Lou Moreno

History Snapshot 26: Back Row: (left to right) Serapio, Petra, Santos, Front Row: (left to right) Adelina, Serapio (father), Candida, Candida (mother), Abram (on lap), Marta, Tana; photo courtesy of Lucinda Elizondo Anderson and Abraham Garcia

Oral History: Tana Rodriguez Castillo

Tana was a daughter of Candida. Norma Ramirez Banks remembered her mother, Herminia Castañon Ramirez, talking to Tana a least once a year.

A younger cousin of Tana commented that Tana was very generous and would spoil them by buying them things.

Tana was described by her great granddaughter as a feisty woman who liked to joke around. She and her husband, Julio Castillo, had a pomegranate tree in the yard and always ate bologna sandwiches.

"My dad remembers she would drive their station wagon around on Sundays and "church nights" to pick up all the nieces and nephews for services. They went to El Golgota church on Vine St. in San Antonio. When my father was young, his mother (Tana's sister Petra) had stomach cancer, and Tana would take her to doctor's appointments and took care of her. After she died, it was just dad and his father until dad's sophomore year, when his dad died of a heart attack. My dad's grandfather and namesake wanted dad to move back to La Vernia to live with him and presumably help out on the large farm he owned. Tana would have none of it and persuaded him that dad should go live with her and Julio, who had two boys of their own close in age and familiar to him. They took him in so he could attend high school, and he stayed with them until he was old enough to graduate and be on his own." – Luci Elizondo Anderson

Maria Guajardo

We found Maria when searching through christening records. The christening record lists her date of birth as 21 Mar 1881; she was christened at the Annunciation Catholic Church in St. Hedwig, Texas, on 8 Jan 1882. Nine years later her half-sister was born and named Maria. Perhaps this Maria died young, before 1890.

Francisco Guajardo

We find two birth dates for Francisco "Pancho." He was either born on 6 Mar 1883 or on 9 Mar 1883. His death certificate lists 6 Mar 1883 and his WWII draft registration lists 9 Mar 1883. He is listed as "Frank" on the 1900 census in Wilson County. He is living with his mother and step-father, Jasper Suttles.

Guadalupe County marriage records show that he married Blasa Andrade, the sister of Maria Suttles' husband, Ben Andrada[15]. They had seven children (see list below).

On the 1940 census, they are listed in Williamson County, Texas. Then they moved to Post, Texas, where Francisco died on 30 Nov 1947. His death certificate lists "Length of Residence where Death Occurred" as 1 year. Blasa died in 10 Nov 1975 in San Antonio, Texas.

Children of Francisco and Blasa:
1. Frank Jr (1906 -) married Maria Campos
2. Ysidro (1911 – 1970)
3. Frutoso (1913 – 1995) married Belia Garcia
4. Alcario/Arcadio (1915 - 1997) married Dolores Gonzales; married Irene Pantojas
5. Ernestina (1918 -) married Jesus Valdez
6. Julio (1923 -) married Andrea Valle
7. Lidia (1925 - 1993) married Tomas Martinez

---

[15] Note: The last names of brother, Ben, and sister, Blasa, are spelled differently. Originally the spelling was Andrade, which was Blasa's last name. But because of a typo, Ben's last name was changed to Andrada.

History Snapshot 27: Francisco Guajardo, Jr, Blasa Andrade Guajardo (to the left of Francisco), and some of their family

Elias Guajardo

Elias was born on 2 Aug 1884 or 6 Aug 1884. His death certificate lists his birth date as 2 Aug 1884; Social Security Death Index lists his birth date as 6 Aug 1884. He is listed on the 1900 census as a step-son of Jasper Suttles. In Jan 1907, Elias married Angelita Ramos (younger sister of Urbana Ramos Ramirez). They are listed on the 1910 census in Guadalupe County with 2 children. According to death records, both Angelita and an infant son died of the Spanish flu in October 1918. They were buried in Kuehler Catholic Cemetery that is now called Santa Clara. A great grand niece of Elias thought that he had never married, so it seems that after losing his wife and child so young, he never married again.

A cousin also researching the family tree asked about the Herminda who is listed on the 1920 census with Candida's family. The cousin knew from her father that Herminda was not Candida's daughter but was somehow related. Piecing together information from census records, family accounts, and death records, we discover that Elias and Angelita had six children (see list on the next page). After Angelita's death some of the children lived with Candida for awhile. Herminda, Elias' and Angelita's daughter, was the girl listed on the 1920 census with Candida's family. No one knew the children that are listed on the 1910 census (or had even heard the names). Perhaps they died young.

In the 1930 census, Elias is listed with his son, Elias, in Wilson County, Texas. Elias (the father) is listed as a farmer on a general farm. His WWII draft card in 1942 records his residence as Williamson County, Texas.

Many years later, Elias became ill with tuberculosis and lived in a small apartment at his son's house in San Antonio. His granddaughter remembered that her grandfather as not very tall, but very thin, and with a full head of hair. She also said that he was very quiet when he lived with them. They were not allowed to get very close to him, but her grandfather spent most of his time in his room sleeping. Then Elias moved in with his daughter, Herminda, and died not long after in September 1962 in Dawson County, Texas.

Children of Elias and Angelita:

1. Julio (1908 -) he was listed on the 1910 census; no other info was found
2. Obedion(?) (1909 -) was also on 1910 census; no other info was found
3. Pablo (1911? -)
4. Elias Ramos (1912 – 1987) married Dominga Ramos
5. Herminda (1914 – 2004) married Domingo Hernandez
6. Conrado (1917 – 1918)

History Snapshot 28: (left) Herminda Guajardo Hernandez; (right) Herminda with her cousin, Cande; photos courtesy of Brenda Alvarado

Jasper/Gasper Suttles

Gaspar's WWI draft registration card lists his birth date as 25 Oct 1887. He is listed on the 1900 census with his parents. There is a marriage record for Jasper Suttles and Adela Rabago in Guadalupe County on 29 Sep 1906. But in the 1910 census, Adela is listed with her father and marked as single. She married someone else in 1913.

On Gasper's WWI registration form in 1917, "wife and child" is written, and his death certificate lists him as married. Continued searches do not provide us with the names of his wife and child.

Sadly, at age 30, he died of the Spanish flu days after his parents died of the same in Feb 1918. He was also buried in the Kuehler Catholic Cemetery; now called Santa Clara Cemetery.

Maria Suttles Andrada

According to the Social Security Death Index, Maria was born on 11 Mar 1891. She is listed with her parents in the 1900 census. On

16 Oct 1905 she married Ben (Wenislado) Andrada. They had six children (see list below). Ben died on 15 Feb 1960; he was buried in San Jose Burial Park.

History Snapshot 29: (left) Maria Suttles Andrada; (right) Maria and her husband, Ben; photos courtesy of Ernestine Andrada

After Ben's death, Maria married Ernesto Montez on 9 Jun 1961. In her later years, she lived with her son, Rudy and daughter-in-law, Ernestine. Maria died on 19 Jan 1984 at age 93. She was buried in San Jose Burial Park in San Antonio, Texas.

Children of Maria and Ben:

1. Lucia (1910 - 1941) married Honorato Salazar ( )
2. Luisa (1913 – 1962) married Ramon Rodriguez
3. Juanita (1913 -) married Juan Moreno
4. Candida (1916 – 1917)
5. Consuelo (1918 -) married Isabel Moreno[16]
6. Rodolfo (1920 – 2001) married Ernestine Garza

---

[16] Juan and Isabel Moreno were brothers

Emma Suttles Maldonado

Emma was born on 22 Nov 1892. She is listed on the 1900 census with her parents. Marriage listings record her marriage on 5 Sep 1907 as Emma, age 14, to Samuel Maldonado, age 22; they had 12 children (see list below).

Samuel and Emma lived on farms for many years, but sometime between 1935 and 1940 they moved into the town of Seguin. They lived at 617 Saunders, and later at 406 Augila. They were active in the local Methodist church, La Trinidad Iglesia Metodista. (David Maldonado)

Samuel died on 13 Sep 1961; Emma died on 9 Dec 1970. Both were buried in Riverside Cemetery in Seguin, Texas.

Children of Emma and Samuel:
1. David (1908 – 1984) married Isabel Camarillo (1909 – 1931); married Anita Molina (1916 -)
2. Florinda (1909 - 1997) married Manuel Hernandez
3. Elvira (1914 - 1996) married Blas Tellez
4. Bernabe (1921 -) married Alejandra Alcoser
5. Elida (1927 – 1929)
6. Samuel (1929 – 2006) married Virginia Mendez
7. Elida (1932 -) married Felipe Camarillo (1933 – 1968); married Jose H Vega (1932 – 1996)
8. A child that died young. Name is not known.
9. A child that died young. Name is not known.
10. A child that died young. Name is not known.
11. A child that died young. Name is not known.
12. A child that died young. Name is not known.

Edward Suttles

Edward was born in either 1893 or 1895. His death certificate lists his birth date as 28 Feb 1895. The 1900 census lists an Edgar born in 1893, but no Edward. The 1910 census lists Edward. He married Adela Luna and they had five children (see list on next page). He was called "Tío Wallo" by his nephews and nieces. Lalo is a common nickname for Eduardo. Wallo seems to be a variation of that.

Edward died on 10 Dec 1964 and Adela died in 1969. They were both buried in San Fernando #2 Cemetery in San Antonio, Texas.

Children of Edward and Adela:

1. Francisco (1917 – 1982) married, then divorced Maria Flores
2. Adelfino (1917 -)
3. Pablo (1922 – 1923)
4. Alejandro (1927 – 1963) never married
5. Mary (1932 -)

8

Manuela, (1860 – before 1880)

When researching you sometimes run across people for whom information is not available or impossible to find. It is like reading a story with no ending. Manuela is one of those people.

Manuela was christened on 18 Jun 1860 in Sagrario Metropolitano, Saltillo, Coahuila, Mexico. Searching page by page through civil and Church death records, we find no death record for her. She was about 10 years old when the family traveled to Texas. It is possible that she came to Texas and married before 1880, but we find no marriage record. If she came to Texas, but died before 1880, there would be no record of her death in Texas, since death records were not required until 1903.

9

Josefa, (1862 – before 1920)

One must not overlook civil records when researching in Mexico. Many have not yet been indexed, but scanning page by page can sometimes garner valuable information. That is how Josefa was found; otherwise, we'd only know about Mariana.

In our earlier search we found that a Mariana, daughter of Jesus Ramires and Maria de Jesus Perales, was christened in Sagrario Metropolitano in Saltillo, Coahuila, Mexico, on 19 March 1862. But by scanning page by page through civil records (because they are not yet indexed), we find a civil birth record for a Josefa in Saltillo dated the same day. Josefa is the name listed on census records, but the name Mariana never appears again. There is no indication on either record of twins.

A Josefa or Josefin is listed on the census records for 1880, 1900, and 1910. In 1880, she is listed with her parents; in 1900 she is listed with her brother, Jesus; in 1910 she is listed with her niece, Candida Torres Rodriguez. She is always listed as single.

In the marriage index for Guadalupe County, there is a marriage license issued to Epetacio Garza and Josefa Ramirez on 30 Dec 1881. There is a note that it was never returned. On 24 Jan 1883, there is a marriage listed for a Petasio Garcia to Josefa Raminso. In 1894, Epetacio married Josefa Cassanova in Wilson County, Texas. Was Josefa Ramirez married for only a short time?

Search after search produced no death certificate. We still do not know when Josefa died. She is not found on the 1920 census with any of her family members. It is likely that she died before 1920. Did she also die of the Spanish flu in 1918?

10

Austacio, (1864 – 1929)

Names for Austacio varied. Some grandchildren remembered his name as Eustacio, the Spanish version of Eustace. They said he was often called Stacio and it sounded like "Stacho." Other descendants knew his name as Anastacio, but that he was called Austacio most of the time. Lacking the christening and civil birth records for him, there is no recorded confirmation of what he was named at birth. The cemetery record and death certificate list his name as Anastacio. Most census records list some version of Austacio (sometimes spelled Ostacio). In this book, I refer to him as Austacio because that appears most often.

Austacio was born in 1864 according the 1880 census. His great granddaughter had his birth year recorded as 1865. We are not able to locate a christening record, but when searching, we discover that some records from those years are missing. He is listed with his parents on the 1880 census. On 3 Sep 1885 in Wilson County, Texas, he married Isabel Alfaro. They had nine children: Lidia, Isabel, Fidencio, Eliseo (Julian), Alfredo, Luisa, Indalecio, Alexander, and Rebecca (see sections in this chapter).

We can track their moves by the censuses and family stories. They are listed in Guadalupe County on the 1900 and 1910 censuses and listed in Dallas on the 1920 census. After leaving Guadalupe County, they lived in Dallas, New Orleans, and Detroit. When Austacio was only 64, his wife Isabel and his son, Fidencio, died in Feb 1929 in Detroit. One great grandchild thought that Isabel was visiting Texas when she died, but was buried in Detroit. I was told that Fidencio died first and when Isabel heard the news of her son's death, she had a heart attack. Her death certificate lists "cardiac failure" as the cause of death. Fidencio died on 19 February 1929. Isabel died a day later on 20 Feb 1929. Austacio died shortly after on 12 March 1929. His cause of death is listed as "Lung Abscess" Others said that they thought all three died of influenza; there was an influenza epidemic in the winter of 1928-1929. Austacio's son, Julian, a Baptist minister officiated the funerals for his brother, mother, and father all within a month. All three were buried in Woodmere cemetery in Detroit, Michigan in unmarked graves. The map of the cemetery noted the graves, but there are no headstones.

History Snapshot 30: Austacio and family; photo courtesy of Michelle Perez Bolanos

Austacio and Isabel had nine children. Seven of them are included in the above photo. The child in Isabel's lap is likely Indalecio who was born about Mar 1900. This photo probably dates to 1901.

Oral History: An Overwhelming Grief

Yolanda Ramirez Amado, a granddaughter of Austacio, was 6 years old in 1929. She remembered her grandfather's funeral and how her father lifted her up so that she could see her grandfather laid to rest. She also remembered her mother talking about how close to one another the deaths were and about "Tía Purita" (Pura, Fidencio's wife) and her immeasurable grief.

History Snapshot 31: Austacio with his Zapata granddaughters, Amparo (left), Oralia (on lap), and presumably Raquel (right); photo courtesy of Michelle Perez Bolanos

Lidia Ramirez Urias

Lidia was born on 23 Jan 1887 in Guadalupe County, Texas. She is listed with her parents in the 1900 census. On 7 Oct 1905 she married Valeriano Urias in Guadalupe County. They had five children (see list below). About 1924, Valeriano left Lidia, and she had to care for her young family alone. Lidia and her children lived in Seguin, San Antonio, Dallas, Chicago, Houston, and Indiana. Lidia died on 1 May 1968 in Chicago, Illinois.

Valeriano stayed in San Antonio and died in 1937. His granddaughter remembered driving by the two-room house (which still stands remodeled) that Valeriano and his 2nd family occupied in San Antonio after he left her grandmother Lidia.

Children of Lidia and Valeriano:
1. Genoveva (1906 – 1978) married Juan Frayre Velasco (1899 - 1981)
2. Eliu "Lee" (1909 – 1977) married Marcelina Navarrete (- 1969); married Anita Martinez (- 2009)
3. Consuelo (1911 -) married, then divorced Benito Olalde ( ); married Cruz Mendoza ( )
4. Elida (1914 – 1918)
5. Rogelio "Roy" (1915 – 2008) married Irene Aguirre ( )

Oral History: Visits from Family

A granddaughter of Lidia's remembered Indalecio, Alejandro, and Alfredo visiting her family while the family lived in Chicago from the summer of 1942 to the summer of 1943. She doesn't remember much about the visit – only that they were dressed up, sat in the kitchen, and smoked.

History Snapshot 32: Four generations – Raquel Velasco is the baby, Genoveva (Urias) Velasco standing, to her right is grandmother Lidia (Ramirez) Urias and Isabel (Subia) Alfaro is the great grandmother on the left

Among the photos that belonged to my grandma and Aunt Linda was a photo of Iglesia Metodista in Chicago, Illinois, dated 1942. We didn't recognize anyone in the photo. The back of the photo was written in Spanish and noted that family members were marked with an X. I posted the photo on Ancestry.com hoping that someone researching the same family would recognize someone. I contacted another Ancestry.com member, discovered we were researching the same family, and he sent me the information about the photo. It is still hard to believe that we were able to connect and identify this group. Some of the younger ones he identified in the photo are still alive and contributed information for this history.

History Snapshot 33: Iglesia Metodista Mexicana 1942; photo from my grandma's photos

96

"The Iglesia Metodista photo includes several members of the Urias-Velasco family. Grandmother Lydia Ramirez is pictured middle left (as you look at the picture) and has an X on her neck. Directly behind her is my Aunt Rachel (Raquel) Velasco Ramos Koncewicz. She is smiling. Just to the left of Aunt Rachel is her future husband, Marcelino Ramos. The lower part of his face is partially covered by the head of the person in front of him. Behind and to the right and left of Aunt Rachel are my grandparents, Juan Frayre Velasco and Genoveva Urias Velasco. Grandpa has the grin on his face and his chin is slightly tilted upward. In front and slightly to the left of Grandmother Lydia is my Aunt Alice Velasco Cortez. She has wire frame glasses on. Standing next to Aunt Alice on the right is my Aunt Idalia Velasco Patterson Edwards. Standing to the left of Aunt Alice is my mother Sylvia Velasco. The little girl in front of my mother is my Aunt Lydia (Lillie) Velasco Wacker, in a head to toe parka suit but no scarf on her head. The girl with the babushka on her head is Elizabeth, daughter of Consuelo Olalde Mendoza. To the right of the photo are two of my uncles. The little boy on the front row with his mouth open (looks like he is singing) standing next to a boy with winter hat who is looking at him is my Uncle Armando (Army) Velasco. Just behind the little boy with the hat that is looking at my Uncle Army is my Uncle David Velasco." *(Photo info from David Aguirre and Alice Cortez)*

Isabel Ramirez Zapata

Isabel Ramirez was born on 26 Mar 1889 according to her death certificate. She is listed in her parents household in the 1900 census. At age 20, she married Santos Zapata on 24 Jan 1910 in Guadalupe County, and they had four children (see list below). Isabel died on 2 Feb 1918 at age 28 of pneumonia brought on by the Spanish Flu and was buried in Riverside Cemetery in Seguin, Texas.

History Snapshot 34: Isabel and Santos on their wedding day; photo courtesy of David Torres

Children of Isabel and Santos:

1. Raquel (1911 – 1929)
2. Amparo E (1913 – 1988) married David Torres, Armengol Piña, and Jose Z Hinojosa.
3. Oralia (1915 – 1972) married a Torres
4. Leonel (1917 – 1918)

Fidencio "Frank" Ramirez

Fidencio was born on 25 May 1891 in Seguin, Texas, according to his World War I Draft Registration Card. He is listed on the 1900 and 1910 censuses in his parents' household. He married Pura Rendon sometime between 1909 and 1914. They had three children (see list on the next page). On the 1920 census, Fidencio, Pura, and children are listed in Dallas, Texas. Sometime after 1920, the family moved to Detroit, looking for employment.

Fidencio died on 19 February 1929 at age 37 and was buried in Woodmere Cemetery in Detroit, Michigan. He is listed in the cemetery records as Frank Ramirez. One family member said that he and his parents, who died around the same time, all died from influenza.

In the 1930 census Pura is marked as "widow." She and the children are listed in Detroit, Michigan. The oldest son, Rudolf, is listed as the head of household. He was working as a cook at a pretzel factory. For a time, Pura and sons lived with Pete Ramirez (a son of Ignacio, discussed in Chapter 13), a cousin of Fidencio.

Fidencio's death was very hard on Pura. The grief impacted her so greatly that she spent some time in an institution according to a niece. Pura died in California in 1972. At the time of her death, she was survived by her son Rudolph Ramirez (who died the following year), two grandchildren, and a great grandchild. She was buried in Cypress Lawn Memorial Park in Colma, California.

Children of Fidencio and Pura:

1. Rudolph (1914 – 1973)
2. Richard (1917 – 1968) married Mary G Conaway; married Margaret M Williams
3. Raul/Ralph (1919 - 1972?)

Eliseo "Julian" Ramirez

Eliseo was born about 1893 in Texas according to the 1900 census. He is listed with his family in the 1900 and 1910 censuses. He registered for the WWI draft in 1918 in Guadalupe County and is listed as married. There is no other information about Eliseo. In a search for Alexander, Eliseo's younger brother, we find a 1930 census listing for him living with a Julian Alfaro Ramirez. After more research and a few Ancestry.com messages, we learn that Julian and Eliseo were one and the same.

Eliseo married Ernestina Ramirez (no relation) on 15 Oct 1916 in McQueeny, Texas. Not too long after they were married they moved to Mexico; Eliseo started a hotel there with a partner. While in Mexico, he started using the name Julian. After a while, JA became his nickname, short for Julian Alfaro, his first and middle name.

History Snapshot 35: Julian (Eliseo) and Ernestina on their wedding day; photo courtesy of Abe Ramirez and Sarah Laffoday

JA and Ernestina lived in Mexico for awhile. By 1927 they had returned to the United States and lived in Detroit, Michigan. Julian and Ernestina had 11 children (see list at the end of this section). They are listed in Detroit on the 1930 census. Because of the depression, Julian (and some of his brothers) lost their jobs at Ford. Julian and Ernestina decided to move back to Mexico because Ernestina's family had land in Morelos, Coahuila, Mexico. They even had water rights.

Ernestina's parents and brother also lived in Detroit and decided to move with JA, Ernestina, and family. Two cars full of people started for Mexico. Ernestina's brother, Abie, drove one car;

Ernestina's parents and her young son, Abelardo, who was about three years old, rode in that car. JA drove the other car and Ernestina, and their other children: Johnny, Leroy, Yolanda, Edna, Eliseo, and Audrey rode with him. They left Detroit and agreed to meet in Morelos, but things didn't quite happen as planned.

The car containing Ernestina's parents, her son, Abelardo, and her brother, Abie, made it to Morelos. JA and Ernestina ran out of money and couldn't continue beyond Houston. They contacted her family to let them know. Ernestina's parents told her that it was worse in Mexico and told them to stay in Texas. So Abelardo, Ernestina's little boy, lived with his grandparents in Mexico for the next four years while his parents and siblings lived in Houston.

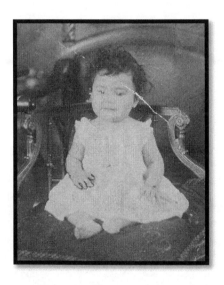

History Snapshot 36: Little Abelardo "Abe" Ramirez; photo courtesy of Abe Ramirez and Sarah Laffoday

They lived in Houston for many years; in Post, Texas, for awhile while Julian pastored a church; and then in Lubbock. They were in Lubbock in 1940 according to the census. They lived in the "ghetto" (the word used by JA's son) where all the Mexicans lived. At that time they could only go in the white part of town if they worked there. One day a man came to their part of town but couldn't find anyone who spoke English; people directed him to JA because he spoke some English. The man worked for a company called Great Western, and he was looking for someone to recruit farm laborers for the sugar beet fields near Denver. During the war, sugar was a valuable commodity not only for consumption but for making chemicals for war. For every person JA recruited he received $100 which was a lot of money back then! JA and family then moved to Greeley, Colorado, where the company headquarters was located.

After a time, they bought a house on five acres in Arvada, Colorado, which is just outside Denver. JA bought a cow (her name was Ela) and two horses to plow the land. They contracted with a cannery which provided seeds for a specific variety of tomato. The family even to this day calls it 'The farm'. After JA and Ernestina died, the farm was sold and the money was divided amongst the 11 children and the church equally.

After they moved to the Denver area, JA and some of his sons and son-in-laws worked for the railroad. JA's son, Abelardo, worked for the railroad until he was drafted.

Oral History: Becoming Baptist

JA and Ernestina were Methodist until one day they were walking past a Baptist church and heard singing. This intrigued JA, and they converted. He also converted his in-laws and then became a Baptist minister.

JA is shown in the photo with his congregation. JA is standing second from the far left. The date of the photo is not known.

JA and Ernestina lived out their last years in Colorado. JA died on 19 Oct 1962 at age 69. Abelardo "Abe" Ramirez heard the news of his father's death when he landed in Panama after flying from his home in Colombia. Once he landed, his sister, Yolanda, who he was there to visit, told him of their father's passing. Together they boarded a flight trying to get to Colorado. They flew from Panama

City to Mexico City, from there they flew to Los Angeles, and then finally to Denver. They attended his funeral, but they had a hard time returning home because many flights were grounded due to the Cuban Missile Crisis. Abe's family was without him in Colombia for almost two weeks while he tried to return home. Eventually they made it home.

Oral History: The Black Chair

Yolanda Ramirez Amado gave her father, JA, a black recliner. That became his favorite chair. He didn't let any small grandchildren sit in the chair because he was concerned that they might pee in his recliner. Below, JA is pictured sitting in his black recliner.

History Snapshot 37: Julian ("JA") in his favorite chair; photo courtesy of Andrea Dahlberg

Ernestina lived another 16 years after JA died; she joined him in eternity on 5 May 1979.

History Snapshot 38: JA with his congregation, JA is second man on the left; photo courtesy of Abe Ramirez and Sarah Laffoday

Children of Julian and Ernestina:

1. Lionel "Johnny" (1920 - 1985) married Josephine
2. Lauro "Leroy" (1922 - 1994) married Pauline Bitela
   married Katherine Julia Rigoli
3. Yolanda Neomi (1924 - 2014) married Julio Amado
4. Edna (1926 -) married Benjamin
5. Abelardo (1927 -) married Leta Mae Hatchet (- 2012)
6. Eliseo "Cheo" or "Ray" (1929 - 2011) married Geraldine Simpson
7. Audrey (1930 - 2009) married Bob Freelove
8. Homero (1931 - 1998) married Gloria Marie Garcia (1930 – 1996)
9. Ernestine (1936 -) never married
10. Olga (1938 -) married, then later divorced Marvin Hutson
11. Hilderlando (1939 -) married Teresa Rojas

Of JA's six sons, five of them served their country in the military. Leroy fought in WWII, Abelardo "Abe" fought in the Battle of the Bulge, Eliseo "Cheo" fought in Vietnam, Homero served in Korea, and Hilderlando "Lando" served in France.

Alfredo Ramirez

Alfredo was born on 18 Oct 1895. He is listed with his family in Guadalupe County in the 1900 and 1910 censuses. Sometime before 1918 he married Herlinda de la Garza. They had three children (see list at the end of this section). They lived in Dallas, Texas, in 1920 according to the census. Their address was 2221 Caroline St. Alfredo was a wagon driver for a transfer company. Both he and Herlinda are marked as able to read and write.

By 1925, they were living in San Antonio. Herlinda became ill with tuberculosis, died in San Antonio, Texas, on 12 Apr 1925. She was buried in San Fernando #2 Cemetery. Sometime after her death, Alfredo married Antolina.

History Snapshot 39: (left) Alfredo Ramirez; (right) Alfredo and Herlinda Ramirez; photos courtesy of Michelle Perez Bolanos

History Snapshot 40: Alfred an Antolina Ramirez (2nd wife), Rene (?), Minerva, Helen, Miguel and Manuel Ynosencio; photo courtesy of Michelle Perez Bolanos

History Snapshot 41: Minerva; photo courtesy of Michelle Perez Bolanos

Alfredo and Antolina had one son, Rene Ramirez, and they lived in Chicago, Illinois. Antolina passed away in Chicago in 1973; Alfredo died on 18 May 1975 at age 79. His last residence was in Chicago according to the Social Security Death Index, but some people mentioned that he moved to Texas and lived near Houston after Antolina died.

Children of Alfredo and Herlinda:

1. Minerva (1918 – 1920)
2. Alfredo, Jr (1920 – 1999) married Janie Perales, then Antonia (or Antionette)
3. Minerva (1921 – 1995) married Miguel Pantoja Ynosencio

Children of Alfredo & Antolina

1. Rene Ramirez

Luisa Ramirez Muñoz

Luisa was born about Nov 1897 according to the census. She is listed with her parents in Guadalupe County in the 1900 and 1910 censuses. According to her niece, she married a Muñoz. Searching we find birth records and death records for children of Luisa Ramirez and Agustin Munoz in San Antonio, Texas. Dates range from 1920 to 1925. Of the three children listed on birth certificates, two died within the first year of life. Only a Maria, born on 3 Nov 1920, has a birth certificate but no death certificate. Is this the correct family? It is hard to know. No records we find confirm the family link or list parents' names.

Indalecio Ramirez

Indalecio was born about Mar 1900 according to the 1900 census. He is listed with his family on the 1900, 1910, and 1920 censuses and is marked as "single." In the 1930 census, he is listed in the household of his uncle, Fidencio Alfaro, in San Antonio, Texas. After multiple searches we find a death record for him. He died in Chicago, Illinois, on 22 Oct 1960. He is listed as "widowed."

His niece remembered that he visited her family when they lived in Detroit; she was very young then. She wasn't sure if he ever married. His nephew remembered that Indalecio would go to Colorado (the Denver area) to work in the fields and described his uncle as a "good guy."

Alejandro "Alex" Ramirez

Alejandro "Alex" was born on 11 Feb 1902 according to his death certificate. He is listed with his family in the 1910 and 1920 censuses. His niece remembered him visiting often during the time they lived in Detroit, and remembered other visits when they lived in Lubbock and Colorado.

Alex is listed in his brother's household in Detroit in the 1930 census. He lived in Houston for awhile and while there married Rebecca Aguirre. The marriage was officiated by his brother, Julian Ramirez. The marriage to Rebecca was short-lived, lasting only about 30 days.

Alex is listed on the 1940 census, living in Houston with his sister, Rebecca, and her children. He is marked "widow." One of his nieces remembers meeting him in California when she was a young girl. At the time, he was married to a Hazel.

Looking at the death certificate, we learn that Alex worked as a machine operator for Imperial Eastman Co. and died in San Antonio on 12 July 1968 at age 66. His death certificate also lists a wife, Ernestina. He was buried in San Fernando #2 Cemetery in San Antonio, Texas.

Rebecca Ramirez

Rebecca was born about 1908 according to the censuses. She is listed with her family in the 1910 and 1920 censuses. A niece remembered the name and that Rebecca lived in Houston at the same time Julian and his family lived in Houston.

After unsuccessful searches, we are about to give up thinking that there is no more information to be found about Rebecca, but then we find the 1940 census that shows her living with her brother, Alex. There are two children listed on the census with them: Louise, age 9, and Eglantina, age 2. Rebecca is listed as "single" on that census. There are also two birth records in the same time period in Harris County, Texas, (their place of residence) with Rebecca Ramirez listed as the mother, but no father listed. Those children are: Jeanette and Oscar. It is unknown if they are the children of our Rebecca. Thanks to a little leaf on Ancestry.com, we found more info about Eglantina.

Children of Rebecca

1. Jeanette? (1930 –)
2. Louise (1931 –)
3. Oscar? (1935 –)
4. Eglantina "Tina" (1938 –) married Rito Gonzalez (1934 – 1995)

11

Gregorio, (1866 – 1868)

Birth and death records may provide more information than just names and dates. One of the records for Gregorio gave information about where the family lived.

There is a christening record for a Gregorio christened in Saltillo, Nuevo León, Mexico, in May 1866. He died of a fever on 21 June 1868 and it is recorded in the civil records of Saltillo. His death record gives the families' location as Meson de Belen. Little information is available online about Meson de Belen, but it was near the center of town, not on the outskirts.

12

Estefana Losano, (1867 – 1957)

Genealogy records are like puzzle pieces; sometimes you have a group of pieces that doesn't look like there is any way they will fit together. That is the case for Estefana. We find several records with the name Ramirez, and some others with the name Losano, but they are clearly the same person. There is a way that all the pieces fit, but it isn't obvious at first.

Estefana is listed on the 1880 census as a daughter. Her birth year varies on census records: 1867, 1854, 1869, and 1870. According to information that passed down through the family, Estefana was a young Indian girl that was adopted in Mexico by Jesus and Jesusa. They brought her with them to Texas and raised her as a daughter.

There is a christening record in Saltillo for an Estefana Losano born to Felisiano Losano and Refugio Sauceda dated 4 Aug 1867. It is possible that this is our Estefana.

Guadalupe County marriage records show that on 13 Feb 1881, Estafana Ramirez married Lucio Guajardo (see the chapter on Associated Families for more info about the Guajardo family). Estefana was about 14 years old; Lucio was 23. They had two children: Silvano & Mariana (see sections on next page). Lucio presumably died before Oct 1890. On 17 Oct 1890 in Guadalupe County, Estefana married Valentine Arispe. They had five children: Lucian, Josefa/Rosa, Cooca, Crescenio, and Joe (see sections in this chapter). The family is listed on the 1900 census in Guadalupe County.

About 1904, Estefana married Santiago Reyna. They had four children: Refugia, Josefina, Leandro, and Osina (??) (see sections in this chapter). She and Santiago are listed in Guadalupe County on the 1940 census.

On the death certificates of her children, she is listed as Estefana Losano. She is listed as Ramirez on census records and on marriage records. Her adoption explains the variation in last name; knowing she was adopted allows all the pieces to fit together.

Estefana was widowed in 1951, and then six years later she died on 16 May 1957. Her death certificate lists her birth date as 15 July 1883 (She had shed 16 years!) and lists her age as 78. But she was really 89 years old. She was buried in Panteon San Lorenzo Cemetery in Atascosa County, Texas.

Silvano Guajardo

Silvano was born about 1887 and named after his paternal grandfather. He is listed on the 1900 census. Continued searches turn up no other information.

Mariana Guajardo Reyna

Mariana was born about 1888 in Texas according to the 1900 census. She was named for her paternal grandmother. On 22 Sep 1909 she married Esequio Reyna in Guadalupe County. They had one child, but the name differs on records. There is a birth certificate for Nellie D born on 2 Dec 1919, but a death certificate for Manuelita Reyna (1919 – 1921) also born 2 Dec 1919.

Reading her death certificate, we learn that when Mariana died on 2 Jan 1920 at age 32 in Guadalupe County, she was already a widow. She was buried in Santo Thomas Cemetery in Seguin, Texas.

Lucian Arispe

Lucian Arispe was born in Apr 1893; he is listed with Estefana and Valentin Arispe in the 1900 census and with Estefana and step-father, Santiago Reyna, in the 1910 census. We find no other information in our searches.

Rosa or Josefa Arispe

The 1900 census lists a Rosa born about 1896; the 1910 census lists Josefa, 14 years old. After searching census records and marriage records, we find no more information about Josefa or Rosa.

Cooca Arispe

Cooca is only listed on the 1910 census with an age of 11. We learn that Cooca is a nickname for Ruth, but even knowing this we find no other information.

Crescencio Arispe

Crescencio was born on 10 Jun 1900 according to his death certificate. He married Olivia Maraquin and had seven children (see list below). He died on 16 Oct 1935 in Seguin, Texas, at age 35 after battling stomach cancer; he was buried in Santo Tomas Cemetery in Seguin, Texas.

Children of Crescencio and Olivia:

1. Francisco "Pancho" (1924 – 1939) died as a result of a car accident
2. Maria Carolina (1926 –)
3. Rosa (1927 –)
4. Anita (1929 –)
5. Adelfe (1930 –)
6. Valentin (1934 – 1934)
7. Alena (1935 – 1935)

Joe Arispe

Joe was born on 4 Jul 1902 according to his death certificate. He married Timotea Soto, and they had 12 children (see list below). In 1940 according to the census, Joe was a "woodcutter," and he and his family were living in Austin, Texas.

Timotea died in Travis County in 1971. Joe died in Austin on 3 Dec 1975 at age 73. He is buried in Assumption Cemetery in Austin, Texas.

Children of Joe and Timotea:

1. Vicente (1929 –)
2. Antonio (1930 – 2007)
3. Valentina (1932 – 1980)
4. Viola (1934 – ?)
5. Eugene (1935 – 1998)
6. Maria (1937 – 2011)
7. Guadalupe (1941 – 2008)
8. Janie (1941 –)
9. Irene ()
10. Ofelia ()
11. Virginia ()
12. Felix (1948 –)

Refugia Reyna

Refugia was born about 1904 according to the 1910 census. Her death certificate noted her parents as "Santiago Reyna" and "Estephena Losano." She died on 23 Jun 1921 at age 17 of tuberculosis.

Josefina Reyna Salinas

Josefina or Josefa was born about 1908. She is listed on the 1910 and 1920 census with her family. She married Luis Salinas and had at least five children (see list below). They are listed on the 1930 and 1940 census in San Antonio, Texas.

Children of Josefina and Luis:

1. Guillerma (1927 – 2000) married Julio Jaimez
2. Avelina (1929 –)
3. Isabella (1933 –)
4. Lucia (1939 –)
5. Luis (1945 –)

Leandro Reyna

Leandro was born on 26 Feb 1909 and died on 6 Sep 1925 at age 16 of tuberculosis according to his death certificate.

Osina Reyna

Osina is the name of a daughter listed on the 1920 census. She was born about 1912. We search using that name, but find no other records.

13

Ignacio, (1868 – 1945)

Labeled photos are invaluable to genealogy research. In my grandma's stash of photos were three Polaroid pictures; each had a first and last name on the back. Searching for these names helped uncover information about Ignacio's branch of the tree. Those three photos (of Sofia, Samuel, and Philip) are included in this chapter.

Ignacio was born sometime between 22 Jul 1868 and 4 Aug 1868. The christening record and civil birth record were dated (recorded) the same day – 21 Aug 1868. The christening record lists him as 18 days old, but the civil record lists him as 31 days old.

He came to Texas with his family when he was four years old. He is listed with the family on the 1880 census; his occupation is listed as "works on farm" even though he was only 12 years old.

On 14 Nov 1891 Ignacio married Otila Ramirez (no relation) in Guadalupe County. They had 12 children: Sofia, Samuel, Petra, Felipe, Abel, Luisa, Ignacio, Ezequiel, Otila, Emilia, Gregoria, and Gregorio (see sections in this chapter).

Ignacio is listed in Guadalupe County with his growing family in the 1900 and 1910 censuses. By 1920, he had moved away from the Seguin area and was living in the Houston area. On the 1920 census, his occupation is listed as a "laborer" and the industry is listed as "street." His sons, Felipe and Samuel, are listed as "laborers" in the "cotton press." Abel is listed as a hotel bell hop. Descendants of Ignacio told me that the family picked cotton, and it was hard work, especially in the hot Texas sun.

Oral History: Meeting by the Tree

Ignacio wanted to marry Otila, but Otila was only 16 years old and her parents were not ready for her to marry. Ignacio arranged to meet Otila secretly. A tree was chosen as the designated spot to meet. Otila arrived first and waited for Ignacio. After a short wait, he arrived on a horse, swept her up onto the horse with him and they rode off to town where they married that day.

History Snapshot 42: Ignacio, Otila and Sofia; photo courtesy of Donald Ramirez & Virginia Garza

History Snapshot 43: Ignacio, Otila, and family. Photo was likely taken about 1926; photo courtesy of Monica Green

One of Ignacio's sons (I've heard conflicting stories about which one – Felipe, Samuel, Abel or Pete) heard about job opportunities in Detroit in the auto industry. That son left Texas and travelled to Detroit by "riding the rails" or catching rides in the boxcars of a freight train. Once there, he found a job and worked until he had saved up enough money to buy a house and bring his entire family to Detroit. He returned to Texas, helped pack up the family, and moved them all to Detroit.

Ignacio and family are listed in Detroit on the 1930 census. His occupation is "carpenter." All four sons worked in the auto industry. In 1940, they were still in Detroit. Ignacio died on 9 Sept 1945 at age 77 from colon cancer and was buried in Holy Cross Catholic Cemetery. Otila died on 30 July 1960, also from colon cancer, and was buried in Mount Olivet Cemetery.

History Snapshot 44: Ignacio and Otila with their kids and grandkids taken at the 50th Anniversary; photo courtesy of Monica Green

History Snapshot 45: Ignacio and Otila; photo courtesy of Donald Ramirez & Virginia Garza

History Snapshot 46: Otila Ramirez, Anita (daughter of Emily), and Sofia; from my grandma's photos

Sofia Ramirez Camarena

Sofia was born on 28 Sep 1892. She is listed on the 1900, 1910, 1920, 1930, and 1940 censuses as single in her parents' household. From my grandma's labeled photo, we know that she married a Camarena. Searching for Sofia Camarena, we find a Social Security Death Index listing and a Michigan Death Index listing for her. From those records, we get her birth date and death date.

Sometime after 1940, Sofia married Salvador Camarena. Salvador died in 1952. Sofia died on 12 Sep 1979 just days before her 87th birthday. She was buried in Holy Cross Catholic Cemetery in Detroit, Michigan.

History Snapshot 47: Sofia Ramirez Camarena; from my grandma's photos

Samuel Ramirez

Samuel was born on 25 March 1895. The birth date is listed on the Social Security Death Index and his World War I Draft Registration card. He served in WWI, and then worked for the Ford Motor Company for many years. Samuel never married; he died on 14 Nov 1973 in Detroit at age 78.

History Snapshot 48: Samuel Ramirez; from my grandma's photos

Petra Ramirez Fernandez

Petra was born on 11 March 1896. She is listed as single and at home in the 1900, 1910, and 1920 censuses. On 28 Apr 1921 she married Bernard Lopez in Harris County, Texas. She and Bernard moved to New York. They are listed in the Bronx on the 1940 census. Sometime after that census, Petra and Bernard divorced and Petra returned to Detroit. She then married Leo Fernandez on 23 May 1951, and they ran a dry cleaning shop together. Petra died on 5 Nov 1955 at age 59 after losing a battle with cancer. She was buried in Holy Cross Catholic Cemetery in Detroit, Michigan. Leo died in 1972.

History Snapshot 49: Petra, on left, and her cousin, Carlos Ramirez, on right; from Aunt Linda's photos

This photo was with my Aunt Linda's pictures. On the right is Carlos Ramirez, youngest son of Jesus Maria Ramirez. This is presumably a photo he'd sent back to San Antonio when he lived in New York. The name of the lady on the left was a mystery until I exchanged photos with Ignacio's grandchildren and discovered that it was Petra, Carlos' cousin, on the left.

Philip Ramirez

Philip or Felipe, as he is listed on early census records, was born on 2 May 1898. He is listed on the 1900, 1910, 1920, 1930, and 1940 censuses with his parents. He married Clara Guerrero on 20 Jan 1919 in Houston, Texas. He is listed in the 1920 census as married, but there is no wife listed in the household with him. On the 1930 census he is listed as divorced. In Detroit, Philip worked for the Ford Motor Company.

Sometime after 1940, Philip married Gladys Halleen. They had four children. (see list below) Gladys and Phillip divorced when their children were older.

Philip died on 16 Jul 1988 at age 90. Gladys stayed in Dearborn until she moved to Daytona Beach, Florida, in 2002. She died in Florida on 9 Sep 2004.

History Snapshot 50: Philip Ramirez; from my grandma's photos

Children of Philip and Gladys:

1. Deloris (1950 -)
2. Janice ( ) – married David Dietz
3. David
4. Greg

Abel Ramirez

Abel was born on 14 Jul 1901. He is listed in the 1910, 1920, 1930, and 1940 censuses as single in his parents' household.

He married Teofila "Pila" Garcia about 1940 and they had eight children. (see list below) Abel died on 19 Dec 1969 at age 68 and was buried in Woodmere Cemetery. Pila died on 5 Apr 1988 and was also buried in Woodmere Cemetery.

Oral History: Chicago

A granddaughter of Ignacio explained that at least some of the family lived in Chicago before settling in Detroit. Late one night Abel was awakened by his brother rustling through a drawer looking for something. Philip told him about a guy with a knife that was causing trouble.

Abel went down and told the guy to put the knife away (that was emphasized with a threat.) The guy declined and a fight ensued. The fight ended when the guy with the knife was cut on the throat with his own knife.

The injured man was taken to the hospital and Abel was arrested. When Abel went before the judge, he was shown mercy. The judge allowed him to walk if he would leave Chicago and never return.

So Abel moved to Detroit.

Children of Abel and Pila:

1. Roy (1941 -)
2. Katherine "Katie" (1942 -)
3. George
4. John "Junior"
5. Joey
6. Arthur
7. Frank (1947-1951)
8. Larry

History Snapshot 51: Abel and Pila Ramirez; photo courtesy of Melissa Ramirez

Eloisa Ramirez Ramirez

Eloisa was born in 1902. Her death certificate lists her birthday as 20 Nov 1906, but earlier census records have 1902 as the birth year. Eloisa is listed with her parents in the 1910 and 1920 censuses. Eloisa married Jesse Ramirez (no relation) and they had one child, Fernando.

When Fernando was born, Eloisa did not pass the afterbirth. She developed a severe infection and died six weeks later on 28 Oct 1928. She was only 26 years old.

Jesse and Fernando are listed with Eloisa's family in the 1930 census, but soon after, Jesse returned home to Mexico and left Fernando with Ignacio and Otila.

Child of Elisa and Jesse

1. Fernando (1928 - 1975)

History Snapshot 52: Fernando (on left) with Mary and Pete Ramirez, taken Oct 1956; photo courtesy of Monica Green

History Snapshot 53: Abel, unknown, Felipe, Eloisa, Tillie, and Emily; photo courtesy or Virginia Garza

Ignacio Ramirez

Ignacio was born in 1905. He is listed on the 1910 and 1920 censuses with his parents. He died in San Antonio, Texas, of tuberculosis at age 22 on 18 Jan 1927. He was buried in San Fernando #2 Cemetery.

History Snapshot 54: Ignacio Ramirez, Jr; photo courtesy of Virginia Garza

History Snapshot 55: Esequiel, Abel, and Ignacio. Photo taken about 1913; photo courtesy of Monica Green

Ezequiel "Pete" Ramirez

Esequiel (or Ezequiel) is the name listed on early census records. He was born on 2 Nov 1907. He is listed with his parents in the 1910, 1920, and 1930 censuses. On 13 Sep 1938 he married Mary Hedwig Czepiel in Lucas County, Ohio. They had six children (see list at the end of this section).

Oral History: Winning a fight

Pete was apparently pretty tough and this story relates to that. He got into a fight in front of Tiger Stadium. Police stopped traffic so that the fight could proceed because Pete was fighting a well-known boxer. A crowd gathered and watched as Pete fought and won against the boxer. Story has it that the well-known boxer he fought was Joe Louis.

Pete worked in the foundry at the Ford Motor company where it was about 100 degrees every day. He did that for 40 years. A few people mentioned that Uncle Pete was their favorite uncle.

Oral History: Changing his name to Pete

Esequiel worked for Ford. At work one day, he got into a fight and was fired on the spot. He needed a job, so after he walked out the door, he walked back into the hiring office and applied for a job. He filled out the application as Pete Ramirez instead of Esequiel. He got the job and worked at Ford for many more years. After that, he was called Pete.

History Snapshot 56: Pete and Mary Ramirez; photo courtesy of Melissa Ramirez

Pete and Mary were married for 50+ years. Mary died in 1992; Pete died six years later on 28 Dec 1998. He was 91 years old. They were buried in Our Lady of Hope Cemetery in Wayne County, Michigan.

Children of Pete and Mary:

1. Charles Michael (1939 – 1994)
2. Thomas (1940 – 1940)
3. Marvin James (1941 -) married Elena Olisauskas
4. Dolores (1942 – 1997) married Ramiro Lopez
5. Gerald (1946 -) married Carol Zwinak (1947 – 2010)
6. Raymond Ralph (1951 – 2001)

Otila "Tillie" Ramirez Padilla

Otila was born on 17 Mar 1909 according to the Social Security Death Index. She is listed on the 1910, 1920, and 1930 censuses with her parents. Tillie married Joseph Padilla on 19 Oct 1931 and they had four children (see list below). Joseph, her husband, died on 17 May 1984; Tillie died on 16 Jun 1992. She was 83 years old. They were buried in Our Lady of Hope Catholic Cemetery.

Children of Otila and Joseph:

1. Stella / Heline (1933 -)
2. Virginia (1935 -) married Al Garza
3. Phillip (1936 - 1998)
4. Gilbert (1938 - 1975)

Emilia "Emily" Ramirez Mata

Emilia was born on 21 Apr 1911. She married Camillo Gutierrez and they had three children (see list below). When the children were young, Camillo left after he was "asked" to leave by Emily's brothers at her request. Sometime later, Emily married a Mata. I think his first name was Cheecho. They were married for a few years and then one day, Mr. Mata returned home to find his clothes on the sidewalk. So he gathered his clothes and left. Later, Emily married Arturo Ibañez; they later divorced. Elmer was her last husband. I do not know if she out-lived him, or if they divorced. Emily returned to using the last name Mata. We learn from the Social Security Death Index that Emily Mata died on 21 Jun 2005 in Murrieta, California, at age 94.

Children of Emily and Camillo:

1. Robert (1935 -)
2. Edward (1936 -)
3. Anita (1937 -)

History Snapshot 57: Tillie is second from the far left labeled "me" and Emily is on the far right labeled "Emily"; this was sent to my grandma years ago

Gregoria Ramirez

Sometimes we learn about people only from those that remember them or tell stories about them, and not from records. We learn about Gregoria by talking with her niece. Gregoria was born about 1913. The midwife, a heavy set woman, came to the house to help deliver the baby. After the baby was born, Otila and the midwife were exhausted and laid down in the bed to sleep. When they awoke, they found baby Gregoria dead. She had been accidently smothered in the night when the midwife rolled onto her.

Gregorio "Grady" Ramirez

Gregorio ("Grady") was born on 12 Mar 1915. His birth date is listed on his marriage record and on his death certificate. He married Catherine Alvarez in Indiana on 17 Jun 1937 and settled in Detroit. They had three sons (see list below). Both Catherine and Grady battled tuberculosis. They spent some time in the tuberculosis hospital together.

Catherine recovered, but Grady died from tuberculosis on 25 Jul 1946. He was only 31 years old. Grady's death left Catherine alone to care for three young boys. She remarried and stayed in Detroit.

Children of Grady and Catherine:

1. Richard "Ricky" (1937 – 2010)
2. Donald A (1941 -)
3. Paul G (1942 – 2005?)

History Snapshot 58: (left) Grady's wife Catherine; (right) Catherine & Grady; taken in Detroit in 1940; photos courtesy of Donald Ramirez

Oral History: Visiting Ramirez Family

Catherine's second husband kept her and the boys away from the Ramirez family. So the boys grew up not seeing aunts, uncles, and cousins. However, when Donald was 15, he walked to his grandma's house and visited with his grandma, Otila, and his Aunt Sofia.

14

Plutarco, (1870 - before 1900)

Census records can sometimes mutilate the names listed. On the 1880 census Plutarco is listed as "Blutucko." That name is obviously spelled incorrectly. Keeping in mind names used in multiple generations of the family may help decipher badly recorded names. Knowing that there are two other generations of men named Plutarco, we search for that name and find information that makes sense.

Plutarco was christened on 30 Jun 1870 in Sagrario Metropolitano in Saltillo, Mexico. He traveled to Texas with his family when he was 2 years old and is listed on the 1880 census with his family in Guadalupe County, Texas. Our searches uncover no other information about him.

15

Ancestors

The Catholic Church records in Mexico are amazing. Because of all that the priests recorded, we have information about family in El Potosí dating back almost 100 years before the familes' departure for Saltillo - and even earlier in a few other places. Below is ancestral information for both Jesus Ramirez (Jose Cipriano de Jesus Alejandro) and Maria de Jesus Perales.

Ancestors of Jesus Ramirez (Jose Cipriano de Jesus Alejandro)

Jose Cipriano de Jesus Alejandro is labeled "Espl" (español[17]) on his christening record. However, his parents, Jose Maria Alejandro and Clara Vega, married on 21 Jul 1819 in the chapel in El Potosí and are recorded as "yndio" (Indian) and "mestiza" (Mestisa) respectively. There is a notation "de Los Mimbres." Los Mimbres was a small village in the mountains just northeast of El Potosí. Was it an Indian village?

Jose Maria and Clara had the following children:

- Jose Cipriano de Jesus (our Jesus Ramirez) was christened on 21 May 1820

---

[17] Español means Spanish

- Casildo, christened on 24 Apr 1822, married Maria Dimas Cardona on 28 May 1843 & had 3 children (used the name Alejandro)
- Paula was christened on 26 Jan 1824
- Juliana, christened on 22 Jun 1825, never married (used the name Alejandro for the christening of her 4 natural children)
- Valentin was christened on 21 May 1827
- Felipe, christened on 6 Jun 1830, married Crescenciana Gimenes on 25 May 1851 & had 3 children (used the name Ramires for marriage then used Alejandro after)
- Nicolaza, christened on 19 Jul 1833, married Roman Balderas on 27 Oct 1850 & had 3 children (used Ramires for marriage, but used Alejandro for christening records)
- Lucia was christened on 22 Aug 1835
- Grabiela was christened on 4 Apr 1838
- Agapita, christened on 28 Sep 1840, married Navor Lara on 29 Apr 1856 & had 7 children (used the name Ramires for marriage, but name varied between Alejandro and Ramires for christenings)

Records show that Felipe and family moved to Saltillo as did Agapita and family. They may have moved at the same time and traveled with Jesus and family to Saltillo.

I have not been able to find a christening record for Jose Maria Alejandro. His parents, Jose Maria Alejandro and Maria de Conscucion de la Rosa, are listed in the 1819 marriage record. I haven't found a marriage record or christening records for his parents. It is possible that Ramires was used somewhere earlier and then adopted again, but I haven't been able to find any records that show that.

Clara Vega's parents, Esteban Vega and Alexandra Leonor Cortez, were married on 4 Feb 1790. Their parents' names are listed in the marriage "acta." The record also notes that Esteban was mestizo and originally from "Ojo Caliente." His father, Vicente, is noted as "coyote[18]." The marriage record lists Alexandra Leonor Cortez as "india."

Esteban and Alexandra Leonor had the following children:

- Jose Dionicio, christened on 28 Jan 1795, married Martina Guana on 13 Feb 1821
- Maria Josefa de los Dolores was christened on 7 Jun 1797
- Maria Clara (our Clara) was christened 19 Aug 1799
- Hemeterio Seledon was christened on 10 Mar 1801
- Jose Maria, christened on 20 Sep 1804, married Anastacia Cortes on 9 Sep 1827
- Maria Jacinta, christened on 22 Aug 1806, married Tomas Solis on 11 Jan 1831
- Jose Lucas was christened on 19 Oct 1808
- Jose de los Santos de la Trinidad was christened on 6 Nov 1810
- Juan Manuel was christened on 4 Jun 1813
- Jose Bruno, christened on 28 Jan 1815, married Gervacia Espurga on 19 Jan 1839

Esteban Vega Gutierres was the son of Vicente Gutierres and Bernarda de la Vega.

Alexandra Leonor was christened on 22 May 1772 in El Potosí. Her parents, Domingo Cortez and Maria de Los Santos Barrientos, were married on 19 April 1760 in El Potosí. Their parents are listed in the record. Domingo's parents are listed as Joseph de la Cruz Cortes and Gregoria Concepcion. Maria's parents are listed as: Manuel Barrientos and Petra.

---

[18] Coyote was one of the terms used to describe racial distinction. Each term represented percentages of Spanish, Indian or African blood. Coyote was a mix of African, Spanish, and Indian.

Ancestors of Maria de Jesus Perales

Cayetano married Gertrudis Alejandro on 13 May 1813. Both are listed as mestizos in the record. They had the following children:

- Maria de los Dolores, christened on 4 Apr 1814, married Juan Cortes on 15 Jan 1831
- Jose Cristoval was christened on 1 Aug 1815
- Jose Ignacio was christened on 9 Sep 1816
- Petra Perales, christened on 6 Feb 1819, married Ramon Cardona on 28 Jan 1835
- Jose Longino, christened on 14 Mar 1821, married Maria Antonia Games on 6 Sep 1838
- Jose Nasario, christened on 15 Aug 1823, married Plutarca Lopes on 26 Jul 1841
- Jose Aniceto was christened on 1 May 1825
- Jose Antonio, christened on 19 Dec 1826, married Telesfora Cardona on 8 Sept 1849
- Maria de Jesus (our Jesusa) was christened on 5 Sep 1830
- Juana Perales was christened on 13 May 1833
- Maria Isabel was christened on 8 Nov 1834
- Juan de Dios was christened on 12 Mar 1837
- Maria Catarina was christened on 28 Jul 1839

Petra and Ramon also moved to Saltillo, but dates on records show that they moved after Jesus and family. Their sons, Juan Cardona and Jesus Cardona, moved to Texas at some point. See the Associated Families chapter for more information.

Cayetano was born on 6 Aug 1793 and christened on 25 Aug 1793. His parents are listed as "mestizo" in the record. His parents, Joseph Matias Perales and Guadalupe Gutierres, were married on 14 Sep 1784.

They had the following children:

- Jose Cayetano (info above)
- Maria Eugenia de Jesus was christened on 3 Dec 1796
- Maria Dorotea was christened on 11 Feb 1800 (she must have died very young)
- Maria Dorotea, christened on 10 Jun 1802, married Juan de Dios Jaras on 25 Nov 1820 and then Marcial Hernandez on 30 Jul 1831

Their parents' names are listed in the marriage record. Joseph's parents are listed as Marcos Perales and Bernardina de la Cruz. Guadalupe's parents are listed as Francisco Gutierres and Francisca. No other information about Guadalupe's parents was found.

Joseph Matias Perales was christened on 27 Feb 1768. His father, Marcos Perales, was christened on 12 May 1739 in Pinos, Zacatecas, Mexico. I haven't found a marriage record for Marcos and Bernardina.

Marcos' parents, Leonicio Perales and Antonia Navarro, were married on 15 May 1729 in Piños. Parents' names are listed in the record. Leonicio's parents are listed as Nicolas Perales and Magdalena Cortes. Antonia's parents are listed as Joseph Navarro and Maria.

Gertrudis Alejandro was born on 2 Apr 1796; just 9½ months after her parents suffered the loss of their two-week old daughter, also named Gertrudis. Gertrudis (the second one) was christened Gertrudis de la Encarnacion Alejandro on 15 Apr 1796. She is listed as "india." Her parents, Juan Jose Alejandro and Catarina Gonzales, were married on 30 Jan 1794. They had the following children:

- Maria Gertrudis was christened on 8 Jun 1795; died 22 Jun 1795
- Maria Gertrudis de la Encarnacion (info above)
- Maria Yldefonsa was christened on 19 Feb 1798
- Maria de La Trinidad was christened on 25 May 1799
- Maria Dolores was christened on 21 Nov 1800

- Jose Miguel died in 1809; no christening record was found

Their marriage record lists their parents' names. Juan Jose's parents are listed as Jose Rosas and Ignacia Alejandro. Catarina's parents are listed as Juan Gonzales and Maria de la Paz de Erevia. Catarina was christened on 20 Dec 1773. Her name is sometimes listed as Catalina.

This is as far back as I have been able to take the family lines (with certainty), but the hunt continues.

16

Associated Families

Some members of the Guajardo and Cardona families lived in El Potosí then in Saltillo and eventually Texas. Here is a little information about those families.

Guajardo Family

Francisco and Lucio Guajardo are listed on the 1880 census as farm laborers in the household of Jesus Ramirez. Each of them married a daughter of Jesus. Curious about whether they were brothers; I searched for a Lucio (because it seemed a less common name). I found that Lucio and Francisco were brothers, both born in El Potosí. Francisco was born in 1855 and Lucio in Dec 1857.

Their parents, Silvano Guajardo and Mariana Guzman, married on 13 Feb 1843. They had six children: Guadalupe, Policarpia, Maria de la Luz, Francisco, Lucio, and Luis. Their youngest child was christened in Saltillo in Sep 1866. It seems likely that the Guajardo family moved from El Potosí to Saltillo when the Ramirez family moved and that they made the journey together.

Francisco and Lucio either made the journey with the Ramirez family to Texas, or followed sometime later and joined them in Guadalupe County. Francisco married Petra (after her first husband died) and Lucio married Estefana (the adopted daughter of Jesus & Jesusa). So, for some Ramirez descendants the Guajardo family is part of their family tree.

Silvano Guajardo was the son of Apolonio Guajardo and Maria Josefa de la Cerda. Mariana was the daughter of Ponciano Cesilo Guzman and Maria Lucia.

Cardona Family

Maria de Jesus' sister, Petra Perales, married Ramon Cardona on 28 Jan 1835. Records indicate that they moved to Saltillo after our family moved, but before our family's departure for Texas.

The Cardona's youngest son, Juan Cardona, did move to Texas at some point. We don't know if he travelled with Jesus and Jesusa or came to Texas later. He was married in Texas on 2 Jan 1888 to Paula Aguero. They had eight children: Petra (marked as Patricia on the photo), Alejandro, Eveline, Josephine, Christina, Martina, Joaquina, and Juan. In 1910, a Carlos is listed with them as an adopted son. Eveline (or Avelina) stayed in touch with my Aunt Linda until the end of her life.

History Snapshot 59: Juan Cardona and daughters; from Aunt Linda's photos

Juan Cardona was born in Dec 1861 in El Potosí, then lived in Saltillo. We don't know when he moved to San Antonio. His brother, Jesus, also lived in San Antonio. Their father, Ramon Cardona, was christened in Jul 1855. Ramon's parents were Dionicio Cardona and Maria de la Luz Sifuentes. They married on 8 May 1805.

Dionicio's parents were Pablo Cardona and Simona Martinez. Maria's parents were Jose Antonio Sifuentes and Trinidad Navarro.

Information about Petra's ancestors is available in the Ancestors chapter.

Charts

For those that want to see the family tree, I've included simple charts (they do not include spouses) on the following pages. If you see an error on a chart or have information that will fill gaps in a chart, please contact me.

ResearchingRamirez@gmail.com

Jesus Ramirez & Maria de Jesus Perales
married 18 Sep 1848

Children:
- Porfiria (1849-?)
- Maria de San Juan (1851-1852)
- Jesus (1853-1918)
- Petra (1856-1918)
- Manuela (1860-?)
- Josefa (1862-?)
- Austacio (1864-1929)
- Gregorio (1866-1868)
- Estefana (1867-1957)
- Ignacio (1868-1945)
- Plutarco (1870-?)

Jesus (1853-1918)
- Ramon (1876-1964)
- Leandro (1877-1912)
- Leonor (1881-1915)
- Dolores (1882-1956)
- David (1884-1910)
- Sara (1887-bef1901)
- Guadalupe (?-?)
- Plutarco (1890-1968)
- Josue (1893-1968)
- Guillermo (1895-1955)
- Anita (1897-1922)
- Clara (1899-bef1901)
- Carlos (1901-1988)

Petra (1856-1918)
- Alcario (1875-1946)
- Samuel (1877-bef1900)
- Candida (1878-1956)
- Maria (1881-bef1890)
- Francisco (1883-1947)
- Elias (1884-1962)
- Jasper Jr (1888-1918)
- Maria (1890-1984)
- Emma (1892-1970)
- Edward (1893-1964)

Austacio (1864-1929)
- Lidia (1887-1968)
- Isabel (1889-1918)
- Fidencio (1891-1929)
- Eliseo/Julian (1891-?)
- Alfredo (1893-1962)
- Luisa (1895-1975)
- (1897-?)
- Indalecio (1900-1960)
- Alejandro (1902-1968)
- Rebecca (1908-2000?)

Estefana (1867-1957)
- Silvano (1887-?)
- Mariana (1888-1920)
- Lucian (1893-?)
- Rosa or Joseta (1896-?)
- Cooca or Ruth (1896-?)
- Crescencio (1900-1935)
- Joe (1902-1975)
- Refugia (1904-1921)
- Josefina (1908-?)
- Leandro (1909-1925)
- Osina (1912-?)

Ignacio (1868-1945)
- Sofia (1892-1979)
- Samuel (1895-1973)
- Petra (1896-1955)
- Phillip (1898-1988)
- Abel (1901-1969)
- Eloisa (1902-1928)
- Ignacio (1905-1927)
- Esequiel/Pete (1907-1998)
- Ottia (1909-1992)
- Emilia (1911-2005)
- Gregoria (abt 1913)
- Gregorio/Grady (1915-1946)

150

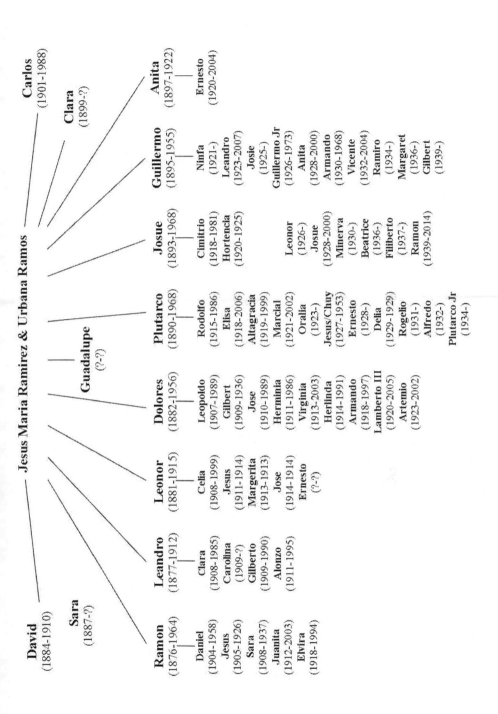

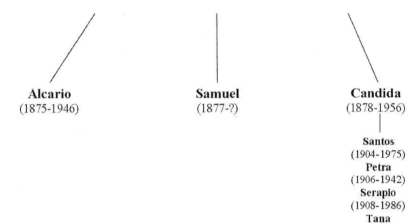

Francisco Torres & Petra Ramirez
married 1874

Alcario
(1875-1946)

Samuel
(1877-?)

Candida
(1878-1956)

Santos
(1904-1975)
Petra
(1906-1942)
Serapio
(1908-1986)
Tana
(1907-1992)
Adellina
(1911-1980)
Martina
(1912-1980)
Candida
(1914-)
Consuelo
(1920-1951)

Francisco Guajardo & Petra Ramirez
married 1880

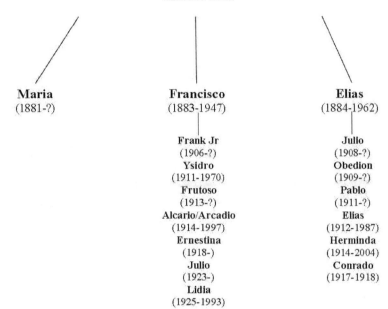

Maria	Francisco	Elias
(1881-?)	(1883-1947)	(1884-1962)

<table>
<tr><td></td><td>Frank Jr
(1906-?)
Ysidro
(1911-1970)
Frutoso
(1913-?)
Alcario/Arcadio
(1914-1997)
Ernestina
(1918-)
Julio
(1923-)
Lidia
(1925-1993)</td><td>Julio
(1908-?)
Obedion
(1909-?)
Pablo
(1911-?)
Elias
(1912-1987)
Herminda
(1914-2004)
Conrado
(1917-1918)</td></tr>
</table>

Jasper Suttles & Petra Ramirez
married 1886

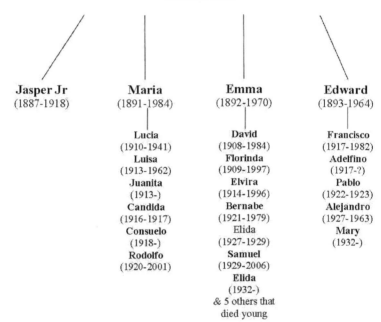

Jasper Jr	Maria	Emma	Edward
(1887-1918)	(1891-1984)	(1892-1970)	(1893-1964)

Maria	Emma	Edward
Lucia	David	Francisco
(1910-1941)	(1908-1984)	(1917-1982)
Luisa	Florinda	Adelfino
(1913-1962)	(1909-1997)	(1917-?)
Juanita	Elvira	Pablo
(1913-)	(1914-1996)	(1922-1923)
Candida	Bernabe	Alejandro
(1916-1917)	(1921-1979)	(1927-1963)
Consuelo	Elida	Mary
(1918-)	(1927-1929)	(1932-)
Rodolfo	Samuel	
(1920-2001)	(1929-2006)	
	Elida	
	(1932-)	
	& 5 others that died young	

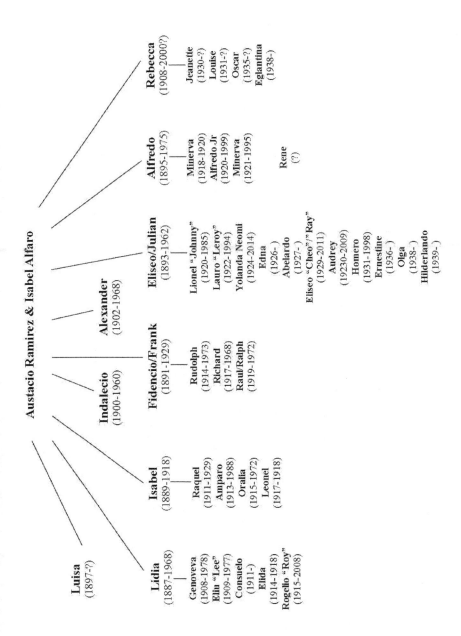

Austacio Ramirez & Isabel Alfaro

Luisa
(1897-?)

Lidia
(1887-1968)

Genoveva
(1908-1978)
Elin "Lee"
(1909-1977)
Consuelo
(1911-)
Elida
(1914-1918)
Rogelio "Roy"
(1915-2008)

Isabel
(1889-1918)

Raquel
(1911-1929)
Amparo
(1913-1988)
Oralia
(1915-1972)
Leonel
(1917-1918)

Indalecio
(1900-1960)

Fidencio/Frank
(1891-1929)

Rudolph
(1914-1973)
Richard
(1917-1968)
Raul/Ralph
(1919-1972)

Alexander
(1902-1968)

Eliseo/Julian
(1893-1962)

Lionel "Johnny"
(1920-1985)
Lauro "Leroy"
(1922-1994)
Yolanda Neomi
(1924-2014)
Edna
(1926-)
Abelardo
(1927-)
Eliseo "Cheo"/"Ray"
(1929-2011)
Audrey
(19230-2009)
Homero
(1931-1998)
Ernestine
(1936-)
Olga
(1938-)
Hilderlando
(1939-)

Alfredo
(1895-1975)

Minerva
(1918-1920)
Alfredo Jr
(1920-1999)
Minerva
(1921-1995)

Rene
(?)

Rebecca
(1908-2000?)

Jeanette
(1930-?)
Louise
(1931-?)
Oscar
(1935-?)
Eglantina
(1938-)

155

Lucio Guajardo & Estefana Losano
married 1881

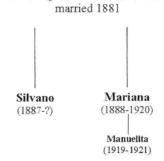

Silvano
(1887-?)

Mariana
(1888-1920)

Manuelita
(1919-1921)

Santiago Reyna & Estefana Losano
married 1904

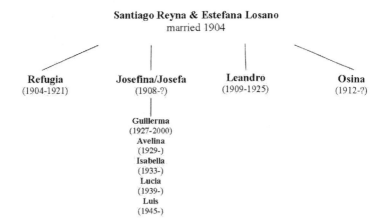

Refugia
(1904-1921)

Josefina/Josefa
(1908-?)

Leandro
(1909-1925)

Osina
(1912-?)

Guillerma
(1927-2000)
Avelina
(1929-)
Isabella
(1933-)
Lucia
(1939-)
Luis
(1945-)

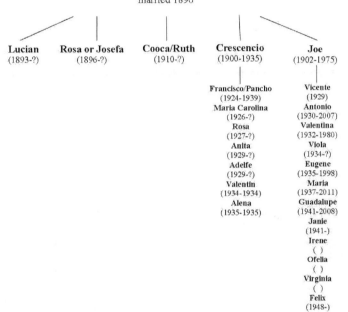

Valentin Arispe & Estefana Losano
married 1890

Lucian	Rosa or Josefa	Cooca/Ruth	Crescencio	Joe
(1893-?)	(1896-?)	(1910-?)	(1900-1935)	(1902-1975)

Francisco/Pancho
(1924-1939)
Maria Carolina
(1926-?)
Rosa
(1927-?)
Anita
(1929-?)
Adelfe
(1929-?)
Valentin
(1934-1934)
Alena
(1935-1935)

Vicente
(1929)
Antonio
(1930-2007)
Valentina
(1932-1980)
Viola
(1934-?)
Eugene
(1935-1998)
Maria
(1937-2011)
Guadalupe
(1941-2008)
Janie
(1941-)
Irene
( )
Ofelia
( )
Virginia
( )
Felix
(1948-)

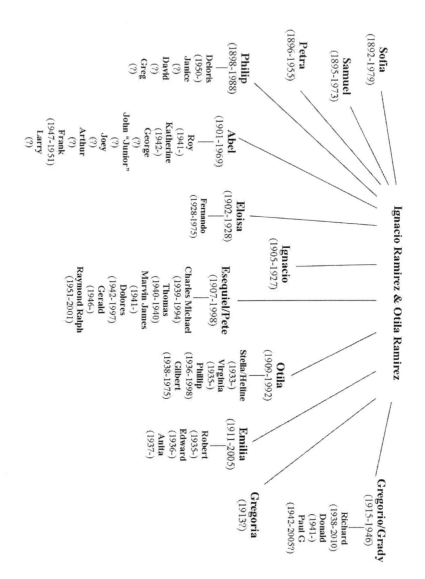

Afterword

When researching, I was not always able to locate sources or pictures for some branches. Hopefully, you will send me stories, memories or photos of your grandparents, great grandparents, great great grandparents, great great great grandparents, aunts and uncles. A second edition might be required.

www.ResearchingRamirez.com

ResearchingRamirez@gmail.com.

Selected Bibliography

Joseph, Gilbert M and Henderson, Timothy J. *The Mexico Reader: History, Culture, Politics*. Durham: Duke University Press, 2002.

Maldonado Jr., David. *Crossing Guadalupe Street: Growing Up Hispanic & Protestant*. Albuquerque: University of New Mexico Press, 2001

Mora-Torres, Juan. *The Making of the Mexican Border: The State, Capitalism, and Society in Nuevo León, 1848-1910*. Austin: University of Texas Press, 2001.

Olivera, Ruth R and Crete, Liliane. *Life in Mexico under Santa Anna 1822-1855*. Norman: University of Oklahoma Press, 1991.

Wasserman, Mark. *Everyday Life and Politics in Nineteenth Century Mexico: Men, Women and War*. Albuquerque: The University of New Mexico Press, 2000.

Genealogy Resources

There are many, many great sites for researching; these are the two I used most.

* www.Ancestry.com

* www.FamilySearch.org

Other sources that might prove helpful are:

* www.rootsweb.ancestry.com/~txguadal/RECORDS.htm
* County Clerk's offices in counties where you are searching. Bexar County has a searchable database online.
* www.FindAGrave.com
* Using Google (or other search site) to search names often leads to information.

Endnotes

*Ramon's poem, A mi Madre: Matilde A Ramirez, translated –

Mothers, Mother, name, sacred name,
Which Christ with his lips pronounced.
Today here, I pronounce to you.
Because love of God is not equaled (?)
Only to you was doubly shared.
For that reason this night before the alter of this humble one
And sacred place, with total respect
On my knee, to say "mother"
And your reverent love, I no longer
See you at my side, nor from your
Lips receive the sweet tenderness,
But if, with my pure innocence,
I see you in the heavenly place!

Who doesn't feel happy
To contemplate the image of his
Mother in whose lips there is no pretense
Boast, in whose heart there is no
Vain sentiment, I for that reason
I much envy those who still
Have that privilege,
Well it is a beneficial treasure
That I from my infancy have lost.

Take advantage of that reward
Those that still have their mother
While that happiness does not end
Enjoy with great satisfaction

To love her with all the heart
And from her counsel (walk toward)?
To see her always with veneration
Well that is the way God orders.

Children this day dedicated to the mother
Give us a very definitive idea
That make of privileged love
That should be for us a lesson of pleasure
And move more our obedience.

About the Author

Pamela Humphrey is a mom and genealogy enthusiast. She lives in San Antonio, Texas, with her husband and sons. This is her first book.

Made in the USA
Charleston, SC
22 September 2015